The India-China Border

The India-China Border

A Reappraisal

Gondker Narayana Rao

MOTILAL BANARSIDASS PUBLISHERS
PRIVATE LIMITED • DELHI

Reprint: Delhi, 2009
First Edition : 1968

ISBN : 978-81-208-3454-5

MOTILAL BANARSIDASS
41 U.A. Bungalow Road, Jawahar Nagar, Delhi 110 007
8 Mahalaxmi Chamber, 22 Bhulabhai Desai Road, Mumbai 400 026
203 Royapettah High Road, Mylapore, Chennai 600 004
236, 9th Main III Block, Jayanagar, Bangalore 560 011
Sanas Plaza, 1302 Baji Rao Road, Pune 411 002
8 Camac Street, Kolkata 700 017
Ashok Rajpath, Patna 800 004
Chowk, Varanasi 221 001

Printed in India

By Jainendra Prakash Jain at Shri Jainendra Press,
A-45, Naraina, Phase-I, New Delhi 110 028
and Published by Narendra Prakash Jain for
Motilal Banarsidass Publishers Private Limited,
Bungalow Road, Delhi 110 007

To

AJIT

ANITA

ARUN

Foreword

OUR RELATIONS with China have deteriorated to such an extent that it is often forgotten that the dispute originated with the Chinese questioning our northern boundary and laying claim to large parts of our territory. Yet a clear understanding of the border problem is essential to grasp the current dimensions and the political and ideological tones of the controversy at its present stage. If, as some protagonists of China claim, our northern boundary has not been fully determined, then it is possible that a genuine misunderstanding lies at the root of the problem; but if the Indian case on the boundary has evidence overwhelmingly in its favour, then clearly the Chinese have been exploiting the issue in order to disrupt relations when it suited them.

Gondker Narayana Rao has spent many years studying the vast amount of material on the subject and served as an adviser to the delegation of Indian officials which discussed the boundary question with Chinese officials in 1960. He has drawn on his knowledge to provide a lucid exposition of the problem, and his work will prove invaluable to all, both in India and abroad, who are interested in the subject.

S. GOPAL

Preface

THIS STUDY was undertaken in early 1964 and was completed by May that year. For various reasons it could not be published immediately. A number of books, including Alastair Lamb's two volumes on the McMahon Line, have appeared since then, and the work has been suitably modified.

I am grateful to friends who have gone through this work and made useful suggestions. The views expressed herein are, of course, my own personal ones.

G. N. R.

Contents

Maps

Note on Source Material

The Report of the Officials of the Governments of India and the People's Republic of China on the Boundary Question gives a detailed list of sources used by the two sides. Besides this, works published subsequently also contain detailed bibliographies. It seems redundant, therefore, to add another bibliography here. However, important references to official papers, particularly of the Foreign and Political Department of the Government of India (Secret External, Frontier and Political Proceedings), and to some relevant published works are given in footnotes at appropriate places.

A large number of maps, both modern and historical, and of small and large scales, have been consulted. Important references to such maps are also given in the text.

1

Nature of the Dispute

WHILE REVIEWING Sino-Soviet relations some time ago, J. K. Fairbank[1] ascribed Chinese behaviour to what he called Sino-centrism—that peculiarly ethnocentric tradition which always characterized China's relations with the outside world. Fairbank warned that while national interests, power struggle, and ideological differences all played their part in determining the course of this dispute, it would be a mistake to stress the role of any one of them to the exclusion of others. Sino-centrism was a mixture of all these and something more.

Fairbank did not elaborate on the meaning of Sino-centrism, but evidently he was trying to draw attention to that unique and distinctive behaviour which is peculiar to China and which is derived from China's historical experience of the outside world and her national response to a given situation. It would be too narrow an interpretation to characterize it merely as nationalism, for unlike other national responses this was something far more positive, assertive, and aggressive.

As with the Sino-Soviet dispute it seems it would be inadequate to interpret the Sino-Indian dispute, wholly or exclusively, in terms of any one of the various factors that have now come to compose it. Whatever its ostensible origin, it is now as much a part of China's ideological and power game as it is a product of her territorial lust. It is, in a sense, a product of China's composite Sino-centric outlook. The question of Tibet and the boundary question were only the early manifestations of this composite attitude. The other aspects which are perhaps more basic to the problem have by now become fully apparent and are hardly disputed by serious students of Sino-Indian history.

[1]*China News Analysis,* No. 483.

Some critics[2] of India's foreign policy have, however, sought to isolate the boundary problem from the other more important factors involved and to suggest that it was perhaps capable of solution by itself. While admitting that it was necessarily connected with questions involving ideology and balance of power, they have averred that the boundary problem was also a genuine one and that any improvement of relations between the two would involve a settlement of the boundary problem on the basis of modifications of the positions taken up by the two sides. They have suggested, therefore, a compromise on the boundary question in order that the present tensions might ease and pave the way for an overall settlement. In suggesting a possible compromise, they have tried to examine historical facts and to find evidence in support of such a compromise solution.

Such an approach, needless to say, suffers from a number of drawbacks. It assumes a certain order of priorities and allots a certain relative importance to the boundary problem, which may not necessarily be correct. Apart from the inappropriateness of dealing with specific aspects of a problem in isolation from the rest and speculating on the possibilities of solution and the effect of such solutions on the other aspects of the problem, consideration of current Chinese policies involves a certain political maturity and a degree of understanding without which one may easily come to grief. Secondly, the assumption that the problem is genuine and that it needs to be settled on the basis of a compromise tends to lead one to seek, select, and arrange his material in a manner which suits one's thesis. It then becomes no longer objective history but purposeful history designed to relate historical events to a particular political situation, the complexity of which one has hardly been able to grasp.

[2]Alastair Lamb, *The China-India Border*, 1964; see also *Far Eastern Economic Review*, 28 February 1963, 18 March 1965, and 25 March 1965. There have also been some papers privately circulated but not published.

The publication of *The Report of the Officials of the Government of India and the People's Republic of China on the Boundary Question* in 1961 has been followed by a number of other independent works which have sought to evaluate the report and to examine the question. Among these Alastair Lamb's work, *The China-India Border*, has acquired a somewhat special reputation for several reasons. First, the Chatham House has lent its name to this publication and recommended it as a "scholarly and disinterested contribution." Secondly, the conclusions reached in the book have the appearance of being independent and objective. They reject as unjustified the huge claims put forward by the Chinese in the North-East Frontier Area of India, but concede the claims over the bulk of northern Ladakh as also over certain small parts of the North-East Frontier Area. In effect, the work seeks to find a meeting ground and a compromise, and for this, if for no other reason, commends itself to some people favourably inclined to such a compromise solution.

The publication of this work has been followed by a more detailed one on the McMahon Line, wherein Lamb seeks to trace the formation of the north-eastern boundary of India against the background of British policy towards Tibet.

These two works necessarily suffer from defects natural to the type of approach adopted therein. Lamb[3] makes no secret of the fact that his intention is to do justice to the Chinese case and to view history through Chinese spectacles. The range of material available to him is limited. Despite his obvious bias in favour of the Chinese case, he makes no use of Chinese sources, a large number of which had been cited by both the Indian and the Chinese sides. He has used pre-1914 British records but has very often sought to reach far-reaching conclusions on the basis of slender and fragile material. This is the case with both the so-called MacDonald Line and the *Inner* and *Outer Lines* as will be shown in this work.

[3]References to Lamb hereafter should, unless otherwise stated, be taken to refer to his work, *The China-India Border*.

A more careful and intensive study of the records and greater regard for evidence contained in local administration records and contemporary travel accounts, items which figured prominently in the India-China discussions, would perhaps have lent greater balance to his views.

The history of Sino-British relations over Tibet and Sinkiang involves an examination of not only British policy from British records, but also of Chinese policy in detail. One would have to go to the origin of things—the nature of Chinese claims in Tibet, their history and their validity. Stimulated by the controversy roused by the India-China dispute, a number of scholars in India and abroad have already been engaged in such detailed studies. If time and circumstances permit, it is the intention of the author also to do this in course of time. In the present work, however, he confines himself to the consideration of such of the material as is relevant to the boundary problem, in its true context and perspective, and to an examination of the historical bases of the conclusions reached by critics like Lamb. Since the main facts of the problem are already known from the report of the officials and the correspondence between the two governments, no attempt is made to restate them in detail.

2

Tradition and Geography

CERTAIN BASIC CONCEPTIONS associated with the India-China boundary, such as its traditional nature and its geographical basis, have been subjects of much discussion and often of criticism and it is natural that this study should begin with an elucidation of such ideas.

Both India and China agree that their boundary is a traditional one; but the Chinese contend that, although the line claimed by them had been formed through thousands of years of history, it could not be based on any abstract geographical principle. The line adopted different geographical principles in different situations. The Indian side had challenged the basis of such an argument and held that in mountainous areas, which were unaffected by political changes, national boundaries tended to follow the watershed line of the mountain ranges. Between India and China, known throughout history to have been separated by natural mountain barriers, the dispute largely centred round the determination of the particular line of mountains which acted as the natural and traditional boundary. Here, in addition to such evidence as the two parties had of actual jurisdictional evidence, one had necessarily to be guided by natural laws of human behaviour. This did not mean that all other evidence would be set aside, but that the validity and possibility of such evidence would be tested against the natural laws of human behaviour in the formation of a truly traditional and natural boundary. The Chinese had agreed that the boundary between the two countries was a traditional one and they could not possibly demur to an examination of such natural processes as were involved in the formation of traditional boundaries.

The precise role that the watershed line plays in the formation of a natural boundary is well known and hardly needs explanation. T. H. Holdich, a reputed boundary-maker, while comparing the effectiveness of the watershed line to other natural features stated: "... of all these natural features, a definite line of watershed carried by a conspicuous mountain ridge, or range, is undoubtedly the most lasting, the most unmistakable, and the most efficient as a barrier."[1]

The principle on which the watershed acts as a barrier is very simple. Where there are a series of mountain ranges separating two political areas, settlements of people inhabiting either side tend to move up only along river valleys. As they move up the valleys, the settlements get thinner and thinner, and by the time they reach the watershed line they get extremely sparse or even non-existent. Between one river source and another on the other side, there is usually a belt of inaccessible and unproductive land which people seldom care or need to cross. Thus, while settlements are definitely checked by the watershed line, other features including mountain ranges and rivers do not necessarily act as barriers. Rivers can be crossed and so also mountains through the passes and valleys cutting across them. Hence the Great Himalayan Range which runs right across Kashmir forms no political or natural barrier until it fringes Uttar Pradesh where it constitutes a watershed. The main range of the Karakoram, despite its great heights, nowhere forms either a watershed or a barrier, for it is cut through by the Hunza and the Shyok and is inhabited on either side by people of the same stock. It is only a subsidiary range of the Karakoram system, namely, the Mustagh lying north of Hunza, which forms an effective watershed and a real barrier. This fact has received due recognition in the recent illegal agreement signed by Pakistan and China regarding the boundary between Pakistan-occupied Hunza and Sinkiang.

In the northern part of Ladakh as in the Hunza area, the watershed line is formed by a subsidiary range of the Karakoram, namely, the Qara Tagh range which directly links up with the great Kuen Lun watershed barrier. The Karakoram

[1]T.H. Holdich, *Political Frontiers and Boundary Making*, p. 147.

pass, about which there is no dispute between India and China, lies not on the main Karakoram range but on a minor range linking with the Qara Tagh. The main Karakoram range turns south-east from a point several miles west of the Karakoram pass and is definitely not claimed by the Chinese as their boundary. The line claimed by them is an irregular one turning south from the subsidiary range on which the Karakoram pass is situated, at a point east of the pass, and then arbitrarily cutting across the river valleys of the Chip Chap and the Chang Chenmo (see Map 1). Indeed, between the main Karakoram range, which has not been claimed by the Chinese, and the Kuen Lun mountains, there is no line of features which can act as a natural barrier. The Shyok and the Chang Chenmo basins both lying beyond the Karakoram are peopled by Ladakhis, and the Qara Qash valley and the great Aksai Chin are frequented by the Ladakhis. The Kuen Lun has traditionally formed a barrier not only between Sinkiang and Ladakh but also between Sinkiang and Tibet. In fact, the eastern Kuen Lun is even now the boundary between Sinkiang and Tibet.

The eastern boundary of Ladakh offers an example of a traditional boundary modified by political changes. Before the tenth century A.D., *Ngari Khorsum* or western Tibet formed a part of the Ladakhi kingdom and its boundary with the rest of Tibet lay at the Mayum pass. This included the entire Indus and Sutlej basins within Ladakh and gave the kingdom a perfect watershed boundary with Tibet. However, after King Ngeemagon divided his territory among his three sons, the Indus and Sutlej basins came to be divided. Nevertheless, except at the points where the Indus and the Sutlej were cut, the new boundary continued to follow the principles of the watershed along the rest of its course. Lanak La separated the waters of the Chang Chenmo from those of Dyap Tso and the spur of mountains coming down from Kuen Lun separated Amtogor from Nopte Tso.

In the Middle Sector, there is a perfect watershed line which has not only served as a clear ethnic boundary throughout his-

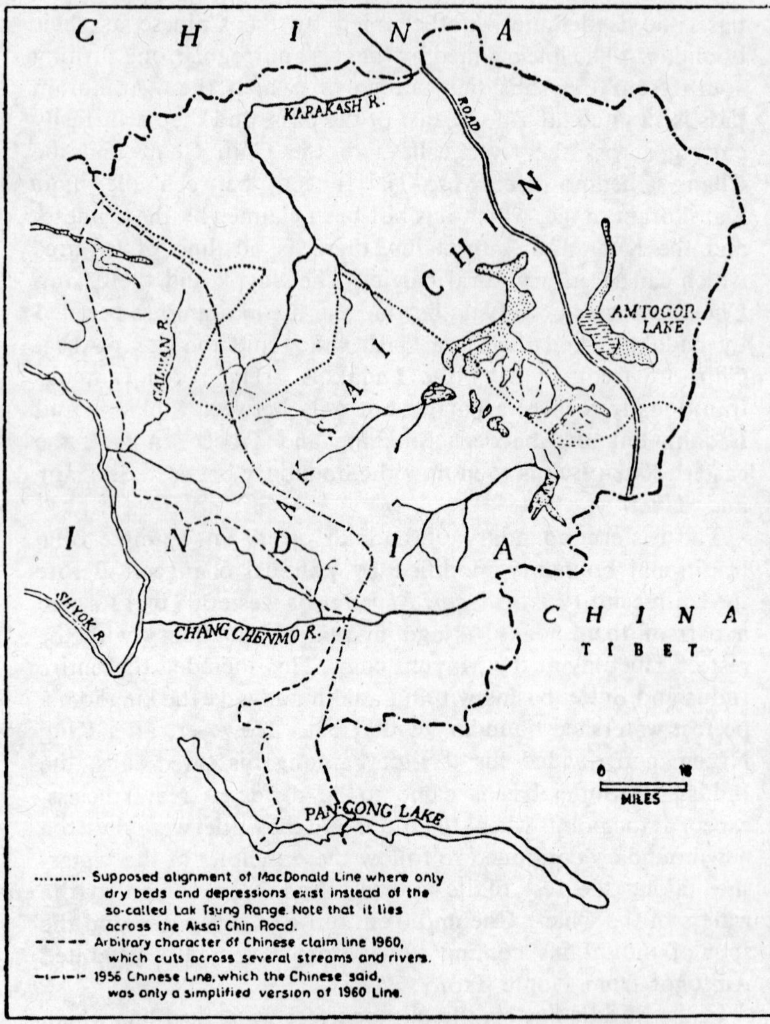

MAP 1. Aksai Chin

tory, but has also formed, in many places, a line separating the flora and fauna on either side.

In the Eastern Sector, it is true, the principle of the watershed has been complicated to some extent by the crossing of the Nyamjang, the Subansiri, and the Dihong, and the resultant easy accessibility of some areas has led to overlapping of cultural and religious influences in a few areas. But this does not prevent the discernment of the traditional limits of sovereignty which continued to be shaped along the major part of this boundary, by the natural processes earlier referred to. The Great Himalayan Range has undoubtedly played its part as an effective barrier separating the Tibetans of Mongoloid stock from the mixed *Lobas* of the cis-Himalayan regions. It is in recognition of this that China has now accepted, without reservation, the main watershed boundary with both Nepal and Burma.

Alastair Lamb[1] has cited instances of overlapping sovereignties and population movements in an attempt to discount the validity of the traditional basis of the Sino-Indian watershed boundary. He has argued that in the Hunza area although the watershed line formed an "effective border," it was by no means the boundary line claimed by tradition, for the Chinese continued to claim sovereignty over Hunza for a long time. Apparently, Lamb thinks that even spurious and shadowy claims can affect the validity of a traditional watershed boundary. The fact that China ultimately gave up her shadowy claims to Hunza and confirmed the traditional boundary in that part provides an adequate answer to Lamb's doubts.

Lamb has devoted several pages to prove that "political boundaries have often failed to coincide with ethnic boundaries." He has pointed out the existence of a Tibetan strain among the people of Ladakh, Nepal, Sikkim, Bhutan, and the NEFA. The Indian side has no quarrel with this argument and has in fact always resisted Chinese efforts to mix up

[1]*The China-India Border*, Chapter 2.

ethnic factors with boundary questions. While watersheds do normally check the movements and settlements of people along the major part of the boundary, they do not altogether prevent the migrations of people which occur periodically due to a number of pressures. Such migrations do not in any way affect the traditional basis of a watershed boundary. The mountains of the north-west, for example, did not prevent the invasions of the Aryans, the Afghans, the Persians, and the Mongols. Such invasions and migrations might sometimes temporarily affect the political frontiers and even leave a permanent mark on the racial composition of the people. But they do not change the national boundaries. In the case of the Sino-Indian boundary, there have been migrations of people but no political invasions, and the question of changes in national boundaries never arose. The immigration of Tibetans in the Mishmi area did not affect the political status of the area and a hypothetical argument that had the Tibetans outnumbered the Mishmis, the area would have come under Tibetan control, has little force.

3

Nature of Evidence

HISTORICAL RECORDS including maps, treaties, official documents, and accounts of travel have played an important part in the India-China controversy, and it is useful to know the nature of such evidence used and the manner in which it has been assessed.

During the 1960 talks, the Indian side were intrigued by the methods of argumentation and the standards of assessment of historical evidence employed by the Chinese officials. Quite often the Chinese used assertions in place of arguments, and sometimes even drew the support of sources of evidence which they had previously rejected as having been drawn from British imperialist sources. Thus, in regard to the Western Sector, while they asserted that their jurisdiction had always extended up to the boundary claimed by them and that they had even held checkposts in the area, they were unable to substantiate the assertion even by a single relevant document. Extensive surveys conducted by Indian parties over long periods and publicized in official reports for nearly a century were branded as "secret" and "sneaking" surveys and, therefore, invalid, while so-called Chinese surveys whose reports and maps had never seen the light of day were brought forward as valid evidence of Chinese administration.

Lamb[1] rightly points out that the rules of evidence should conform to certain standards of veracity, admissibility, and relevance. But he seems to have been unable to apply these rules to the items of Chinese evidence, for the latter were either not available to him or he was unfamiliar with them. He has confined himself to an examination of certain items of Indian evidence which were readily available to him.

[1]*The China-India Border*, p. 41.

MAPS

Dealing with maps, Lamb attaches prime importance to official maps based on scientific surveys. This is as it should be. Maps of the British War Office and other foreign cartographic organizations were cited by the Indian side mainly as corroborative evidence. Although these were not survey maps, they were certainly based on survey maps. Many of these foreign maps, such as Joseph Chavanne's map of *Central Asien*, were cartographic productions of a high order. As for geological maps, they were produced not only as cartographic evidence but also as evidence of administrative jurisdiction. Route maps cannot be brushed aside as of little value, for such maps when prepared by professional surveyors constitute primary evidence.

Among the British surveys of the Indian frontier regions it is refreshing to note that, unlike the Chinese, Lamb accepts the surveys conducted and the boundaries ascertained by Strachey and Godwin Austen as valid. Doubts have been raised, however, in regard to the reliability of Johnson's survey in the Aksai Chin area and the boundary shown by him along the Kuen Lun. These doubts are based mainly on the controversy raised by certain geographers regarding the precise identification and altitude of one of the peaks Johnson claimed to have ascended. The controversy was confined to certain specific points and did not in any way affect the genuineness of Johnson's surveys. Indeed, it was generally recognized that Johnson was a very able surveyor. Dr. Longstaff, one of the authorities, stated:

> It is one thing to say of a "mere mountaineer" that he mistook his position or his peak, and quite another to suggest this of a professional surveyor. As a matter of fact, I believe, no one has as yet questioned Johnson's identifications of the peaks he climbed in 1865 from the Kuen Lun plains.

Longstaff also quoted the favourable opinion of Montgomerie and other authorities regarding the important services Johnson had rendered to geography. Sven Hedin, who summarized the controversy on the question of peak E. 61, conceded that Johnson probably did not ascend the peak, but nevertheless he stated: "This and other facts do not in the least diminish the value of his courageous feat, and mistakes are made even by the best trained explorers."[2] Similarly, Mason says of Johnson:

> Johnson had an exceptionally interesting career, even among his contemporaries in the Himalaya. Born and educated in India, the son of English parents, he had already attracted notice in the Great Trigonometrical Survey before completing the work described above. He was the most indefatigable of observers during the triangulation of Kashmir from 1857 till 1863. His work was in the most difficult parts of the country and more than once he was detached to help other observers in difficulties. In 1861 two of his stations were above 20,000 feet; in 1862, seven. For sixty years four of his stations were the highest triangulation stations in the world.[3]

It is clear, therefore, that whatever doubts there might be regarding certain specific points of Johnson's survey, neither the general value of Johnson's survey nor the fact of his having officially surveyed the Aksai Chin area on behalf of the Survey of India can be questioned. Indeed, no surveyor or geographer has ever gone to the extent of totally rejecting Johnson's survey. The detailed report of Johnson on these surveys, to which Lamb does not seem to have had access, was officially published by Walker, head of the Great Trigonometrical Survey, in 1866.

The boundary marked by Johnson lay along the traditional Indian alignment in the Kuen Lun area, and further north of the traditional alignment beyond Shahidulla in the Karakoram pass area. That was the state of actual jurisdiction at

[2]See Sven Hedin, *Southern Tibet*, Vol. VII, p. 246.

[3]Kenneth Mason, *Abode of Snow*, p. 79.

that time and Lamb has admitted this elsewhere in his book. Johnson can hardly be blamed for representing the true state of affairs.

The surveys of Johnson and of other members of the Kashmir survey missions of 1862-65 constitute basic evidence both of administrative jurisdiction and of actual boundary existing at the time. If further corroboration were required, one should naturally turn to other official surveys of later periods. The Indian side cited corroborative evidence from the reports of the survey parties attached to the Yarkand missions of 1870 and 1874. The total absence of any type of Chinese surveys of or maps for this period provided excellent negative evidence in favour of the Indian alignment. But Lamb ignores these authoritative sources and seeks to find corroboration in the map attached to Drew's work, *The Jammoo and Kashmir Territories.* Drew was Governor of Ladakh and an official of the Kashmir government, but was not by any means a surveyor. Except in the Qara Qash valley he showed the boundary in accordance with the Indian alignment along the Kuen Lun. Drew was careful to note that the boundary represented only his "opinion of what would be defined were the powers interested to attempt to agree to a boundary." This personal opinion of his can be accepted as of corroborative value for the Aksai Chin area, but rejected for the Qara Qash valley as it is unsubstantiated by any other source for the latter area. Neither Drew's personal opinion nor the evidence of his map can any day rank higher in authority than the Chinese Postal Maps of 1917, 1919, and 1933. The latter maps not only carried official authority but were based on, and were consistent with, previous Chinese maps in regard to the Sinkiang boundary. These maps, as for example, the ones from *Hsi yu tu chih* (1762) and *Hsin chiang chih lueh* (1821),[4] were based on old style surveys and careful compilation of geographical material by officials and scholars, and it can hardly be argued that the latter were ignorant on

[4]See Maps 2 and 3.

boundary matters. These works contain detailed discussions on frontier areas. Aksai Chin and the Qara Qash valley which at no time belonged to China had evidently never been surveyed and were, therefore, not included within Chinese boundaries in any of these maps. Such lack of surveys by the Chinese in the frontier regions, therefore, affords negative evidence of great value in favour of the Indian claim.

A clear understanding of the geographical features of the area involved is undoubtedly essential in reaching a proper assessment of the value and significance of maps and surveys in this dispute. Any attempt to simplify the problem by stating that "Karakoram range runs south-east from the Karakoram pass" and that the Chinese erected a pillar at the Karakoram pass "in support of their claim that the Karakoram range was their frontier" will lead to serious misunderstandings in the assessment of cartographic evidence. As has been observed earlier, the Karakoram range turns south-east from a point several miles west of the Karakoram pass and the Chinese certainly do not claim the main Karakoram range all along the northern Ladakh border.

An important aspect which Lamb has failed to consider in the assessment of territorial claims based on surveys and cartographic evidence is the relative value, in terms of legal evidence, of open surveys, the results of which were published, on the one hand, and secret surveys whose results were never published, on the other. The Indian surveys in the Aksai Chin area, for example, were openly conducted for some years and their results published as long ago as 1866. No protests were ever made by the Chinese. The Chinese claimed that they too had conducted surveys in 1891-92 and 1940-41. The results of these surveys had never been published and there is no means even now of judging either the nature or the genuineness of these surveys. How can evidence of such nature be considered valid?

TREATIES

While dealing with the question of treaties concerning the India-China boundary, commentators often overlook the fact that the aid of treaties and agreements was sought only to corroborate and to confirm the already existing boundary and not to establish a fresh basis for it. The boundary had evolved long before the treaties came into being, through custom and tradition. It was hardly necessary for the treaty of 1684 and the treaty of 1842 to specify every detail of a boundary which was well known and in actual daily observance in the Western Sector.

The Chinese side, which had at first apparently accepted the authenticity of the 1684 treaty, later raised doubts about its authenticity chiefly on the ground that contemporary Tibetan works had not mentioned it. It was pointed out to them that this contention was not correct, for the biography of Bsod-Nams-Stebs-Rgyas of Polha had definitely made a reference to this peace settlement. The *Lapchak* and *Chaba* missions, which continued to be exchanged right up to recent times, were originally based on the terms of the 1684 treaty. Neither the existence of the treaty nor the authenticity of its terms had ever been questioned by scholars. Any doubts on these points would only reveal ignorance of authoritative literature on the subject. Luciano Petech, the foremost authority on Tibetan and Ladakhi sources, refers to the treaty and its terms in the following words:

> The negotiations were held at Tingmosgang, and led to a final settlement of the relations between Tibet and Ladakh. The borders, then set, stood unchanged even after the Dogra conquest; the territorial status settled at Tingmosgang has lasted to this day.
>
> The basis of the treaty was the *uti possidetis* principle. Accordingly, Guge, Purang, Ruthog and the regions between the Kailasa and the Maryum-la, occupied by the Tibetans, were awarded to the Lhasa Government, after

belonging to Ladakh for 53 years. Perpetual peace was pledged and a trade pact was also concluded.[5]

The Lhari stream, which was claimed by the Chinese as a boundary point and which found specific mention in the treaty of 1684, is capable of easy identification not only on the spot but also in published works and maps. The Indian side gave the precise location of this stream in terms of co-ordinates, while the Chinese side failed to give its location and thereby revealed gross ignorance and inconsistency in regard to the details of the boundary claimed by them.

The treaty of 1842[6] was concluded at the end of a great deal of fighting in the Ladakh-Tibet border areas. The fighting had been caused by Zorawar Singh's attempt to extend the frontiers of Kashmir up to Mayum pass, the perfect watershed and one time boundary of Ladakh. The attempt had failed and the treaty sought to restore the territorial *status quo*. The treaty did not specify where the boundary lay. But it stated in unmistakable terms· "We shall neither at present nor in future have anything to do or interfere at all with the boundaries of Ladakh and its surroundings as fixed from ancient times...." It went on to emphasize: "We shall not even to the extent of a hair's breadth act in contravention of the terms that we have agreed to above regarding ... the fixed boundaries of Ladakh...."

Could it be that such a treaty drawn specifically to restore the old "fixed boundaries" would allow doubts to remain about the location of the boundary and use the word "fixed" without intent or purpose? Evidently, there were no doubts in the mind of either party regarding the location of the boundary. That is what the great Chinese Imperial Commissioner meant when he stated: "... The borders of these territories have been sufficiently and distinctly fixed ... and

[5]Luciano Petech, *A Study on the Chronicles of Ladakh*, p. 158.

[6]For discussions of this treaty, see *Report of the Indian Officials*, pp. 52-3, 60-2; see also Rose, Fisher, and Huttenback, *Himalayan Battleground*, 1963, Chapter VII.

it will prove far more convenient to abstain from any additional measures for fixing them." Could the treaty be now considered defective because after a hundred and twenty years of observance of the treaty provisions, including those regarding the boundary, one of the parties decides to forget the customary boundary and asks for a fresh delimitation?

Lamb has raised no new points regarding the Simla Convention of 1914. But it would appear that, despite the detailed account which appears in the *Report of the Indian Officials*, confusion still remains. The traditional Indo-Tibetan boundary in the Eastern Sector had first been confirmed through a specific exchange of notes in March 1914. The detailed delineation of the boundary was done on a map of scale 1":8 miles on this occasion. The Simla Convention of 3 July was of much wider scope but provided further confirmation to the Indo-Tibetan boundary. Whether this convention was initialed or signed is of little consequence to the Indo-Tibetan boundary which had already been agreed to in March 1914. What is of importance is that the Convention was ratified by the British and Tibetan governments through a declaration accepting its terms as binding on the two governments. This declaration as well as the map attached to the Convention bore full signatures. The declaration also bore the seals of the principal monasteries of Tibet including the Drepung monastery. The Tibetan Government never questioned its validity and always remained faithful to it. Arguments regarding the non-adhesion of the Chinese Government are of little relevance in this context, for before 1951 Tibet always exercised the right to enter into independent agreements.

The criticism[7] that has recently been levelled regarding the validity of the Tripartite Convention in terms of the Anglo-Russian Convention of 1907 has very little substance in it. First, China was no party to the 1907 Convention and could hardly invoke its assistance. Indeed she never attempted to do

[7]Lamb, *McMahon Line*, II, pp. 506-17, 558.

so. Secondly, the British Government had kept the Russian Government duly informed of the progress of the negotiations with China and actually obtained Russian concurrence before signing the Tripartite Convention. The Russian Government were more interested in utilizing the opportunity, thus provided, for wresting concessions in Persia and Afghanistan than in disputing the validity of the proposed Convention. On the basis of assurances given by the British Government, an informal agreement was soon reached and the British were permitted to proceed with the signing of the Tripartite Convention.[8] In deference to Russian wishes, the British agreed to make some alterations in Article 10 of the Convention initialed earlier. These alterations were conveyed also to the Chinese Government who raised no objections.[9]

The Indo-Tibetan Agreement of 24-25 March 1914 as also the maps accompanying it were presented to the Russian Government on 8 May 1914, and they were told that these documents were of no practical interest for Russia and that they were being presented only for information in view of the friendly relations between the two governments. The criticism that the Russian Government probably did not understand the implications of this agreement has very little basis, for the detailed maps attached to the agreement having been duly presented to the Russians they would certainly have detected the "cession of Tibetan territory" if any.[10]

[8]File SE October 1914, 134-396, proc. Nos. 287, 290, and 303. See Appendix regarding the terms of the agreement.

[9]File SE October 1914, 134-396, enclosure to proc. No. 370. Certain aspects of the validity of the Simla Convention are discussed also in N. C. Sinha, *Tibet: Considerations on Inner Asian History*, Calcutta, 1967, pp. 14-7.

[10]G. Buchanan to Sir Edward Grey, 8 May 1914; see also SE October 1914, proc. 333. Lamb's assertion (*McMahon Line*, p. 509) that the maps accompanying the Indo-Tibetan Agreement of March 1914 were not given to the Russians has no basis. The letter of Sir Edward Grey clearly mentioned "Indo-Thibet Boundary Agreement" which had "been separately negotiated and initialed by the British and Thibetan Plenipotentiaries." Obviously, he could not be referring only to the exchange of letters dated 24 and 25 March 1914 which were signed

Lamb has raised some questions regarding the significance of agreements entered into by the British Government with the frontier tribes. His doubts are understandable, for it is difficult for anyone unfamiliar with the intricacies of British tribal and frontier policies to understand their precise meaning. Some of these aspects have been discussed at considerable length in the *Report of the Indian Officials*, and there should now be no difficulty in interpreting the agreements. The agreement of 1844 cited by Lamb was signed by the Bhutiya chiefs of Tawang and other areas adjoining the Darrang district of Assam. The terms of the agreement leave little room for different interpretations. The agreement stated that in accordance with the orders of the Governor-General, the chiefs would receive a "pension" of Rs. 5,000 and that they would "voluntarily pledge" themselves to abide by the conditions imposed.

It should be noted that most of these agreements were, in effect, undertakings given by the tribal people to authorities which controlled them. That was the normal method employed by the British Government to maintain order and security in the tribal areas both in the north-west and the north-east frontier regions.

DOCUMENTS

Lamb has rightly pointed out[11] that without a certain measure of basic agreement regarding the legal significance of docu-

separately (and not jointly) by McMahon and Lonchen Shatra. The maps were an essential part of the exchange of letters and they alone were jointly "initialed" (actually they were signed) by both the representatives. Indeed one of the Foreign Office records which Lamb himself has cited clearly mentions in the margin that the maps sent to Moscow included those accompanying the Tripartite Agreement as well as the Indo-Tibetan Agreement. This is an example of the nature of pitfalls one encounters in studying documents and the manner in which one may reach wrong conclusions on the basis of inadequate or uncritical study of such documents.

[11]Lamb, *op. cit.*, p. 55.

ments, discussions could be fruitless. Indeed, the Indian side found it extremely difficult to explain to their Chinese counterpart that monastic dues collected by the Drepung and Tawang monasteries and taxes collected from private estates in the Tawang area by Tibetan officials were no valid evidence of temporal jurisdiction by Tibet. Even authoritative opinions given by China's own representatives at the Simla Conference to the above effect failed to convince the Chinese side.

NARRATIVES OF TRAVEL

Travel accounts should certainly be treated with care and examined critically. When so treated, however, they constitute evidence of great value regarding the actual state of affairs on the ground and of effective jurisdiction. Such evidence submitted by the Indian side established the validity of Indian claims not only in the Lanak pass area but also in the regions of Yangi Dawan (in the Kuen Lun), Niagzu and Demchok (east of Ladakh), Shipki pass (Himachal Pradesh), Niti pass (Uttar Pradesh), and along the main Himalayan range (in the Eastern Sector). It is the political argument resorted to by the Chinese, that most of the travellers cited were of British nationality, which made careful appreciation of this type of evidence difficult during the 1960 talks.

In any discussions either of boundary or other matters, it is essential not only to employ uniform standards of assessment of evidence but also to base arguments on facts and reason. Mere assertions that the Chinese boundary always lay across the Chip Chap river, the Galwan river, the Chang Chenmo river, and at the Kong-ka pass, will carry no weight whatsoever if no evidence is produced to support such assertions. There is not a single reference either in the administrative or travel records produced by either side to support these particular assertions of "traditional alignment" claimed by the Chinese.

4

Tibet and Sinkiang in British and Chinese Policies

INDIA and her non-Chinese critics are in agreement regarding the nature of past Chinese policies in Tibet and Sinkiang—the two areas which, until the present Chinese Government came to power, enjoyed varying degrees of autonomy and even independence. For example, Lamb[1] gives a geopolitical interpretation of Chinese policies towards these areas and notes, rightly, that the Chinese have always tended to consider their own security as being dependent on an aggressive policy towards these two areas and that in this respect the present communist rulers are only following in the footsteps of the Han and Tang emperors. Indeed, the present rulers have gone further for, while their predecessors had never succeeded in establishing direct administration in Tibet, they are now engaged in a policy of incorporation and colonization of Tibet. This policy which was initiated by the Manchus through Chao Erh-feng in the early years of the present century has been brought to fruition by the present regime and has given rise to the Sino-Indian boundary question.[2]

It is hardly possible to find fault with Lamb's thesis except for the fact that, in the subsequent treatment of the problem, he tends to place Chao Erh-feng's military activities (1905-10) and the "liberation of Tibet" (1950-51) on the same footing as the extension of regular Indian administration in a backward area which was always under Indian control. What were the relative legal and political positions of Tibet and the NEFA areas? Even assuming that the tribal areas of NEFA enjoyed autonomous status, does the incorporation of such autonomous backward areas into a State which controlled them compare

[1]*The China-India Border*, Chapter 3.
[2]*Ibid.*, p. 31.

with the annexation of a regularly constituted State like Tibet, with a distinct territory and nationality, by another State claiming to be its sovereign but disowned by the former State? These are questions which are perhaps not directly concerned with the determination of a traditional boundary, but certainly relevant in the consideration of motivations which Alastair Lamb perhaps intended but failed to establish in his work.

In regard to Sinkiang again Lamb draws a parallel between Chinese, Russian, and British advances in the nineteenth century and considers the Sino-Indian boundary a direct result of such advances. He does not state what the position was before these advances. Was there a state of vacuum? And if there was no vacuum, what was the territorial position before the advances commenced? Once the territorial position or the "traditional" national boundary is traced, it would be easy to determine who advanced against whom and whether there was any advance at all. Lamb asserts that the present-day state of Kashmir was created through nineteenth century historical evolution, but ignores the fact that whatever its various political transformations it continued to be Indian territory through the successive periods of the Mauryas, the later Hindu kings, the Mughals, and the Sikhs. And as for the traditional limits of national territories, material is not lacking. Even Chinese literature provides abundant proof of the limits of Chinese territory. An examination of such material was essential before dealing with the so-called imperialist advances and evolution of the boundaries in the nineteenth century. Lamb has failed to do this.

Lamb has attempted a survey of the political relations that China and Tibet had with Nepal, Bhutan, and Sikkim, and speculated on the possibility of China exploiting her former shadowy claims on these States. He admits, however, that these claims have worn so thin that no court of international law would uphold them today. This question has so little connection with the question of Sino-Indian boundary and is of such theoretical value that it is hardly necessary to deal with it in the present context.

5

Ladakh's Eastern Boundary, 1864

BETWEEN 1846 and 1864, the Ladakh-Tibet boundary was visited by a number of British officials, and valuable data were collected regarding the location of the customary boundary. By a careful evaluation of this data, the Government of India could have at this time, had the need arisen, specified the line of Ladakh-Tibet boundary with great precision. But such an evaluation was seldom done and although most officials traced the boundary correctly along the watershed range running parallel to the river Indus, gross blunders were committed regarding the alignment in the Pangong and Demchok areas. This was apparently due to the unfamiliarity of some of the British officials with the traditional and treaty basis of the boundary, and to their mistaking local disputes such as pasture disputes with boundary disputes. Great care should, therefore, be taken in examining these accounts critically and in relating them to facts already known, before accepting them as correct.

EARLY TRAVEL ACCOUNTS

Among the accounts of early travellers, those of Desideri (1715-16) and Fraser (1820) are certainly of great value both as evidence which is in agreement with facts already known and as providing a basis against which the credibility of later evidence could be tested. Desideri states that he reached the "confines" of Ladakh and the frontier town of Tashigong on 7 September 1715. Since the boundary of Ladakh in this particular sector was specifically fixed only about thirty years prior to this at the Lhari stream in the neighbourhood of Demchok, it is normal to assume that it was to this boundary that Desideri refers when he mentions the confines of Ladakh.

Any other inference would not only be without basis but would conflict with facts already known.[1]

Fraser, who travelled in the Himalayas in 1815 and collected detailed information about the routes, states clearly and specifically that Demchok lay in Ladakh and Tashigong in China.[2]

As compared to the evidence of Desideri and Fraser (Pattee Ram), the evidence of Moorcroft, to which Lamb seems to attach considerable importance, provides no precise or specific information and is, therefore, of little value for the Ladakh-Tibet boundary. Moorcroft's travels were confined to the interior of Ladakh and the farthest point he reached was the Chushul valley. His companion, George Trebeck, travelled some distance further south up to Chibra on the Indus, but not up to the boundary. Any reference to Demchok as Tibetan territory either by Trebeck or Moorcroft would naturally be based on hearsay information, and should be rejected as of no value particularly because it conflicts with known historical facts and other contemporary as well as subsequent evidence of greater value.[3]

Moorcroft's evidence regarding the northern boundary of Ladakh is, however, of greater value, for although he did not visit this region, unlike the eastern boundary of Ladakh where specific points were involved, this Ladakh-Khotan

[1]Demchok was a customary camping place and its distance from Tashigong is more than 20 miles. If it is assumed that the boundary lay north of Demchok, then we would have to explain Desideri's "reaching" that border and passing Demchok without the normal halt and reaching Tashigong also (which would be not less than 30 miles from the assumed border) on the same day. Such an assumption finds no basis in Desideri's account.

[2]The fact that Fraser obtained his information regarding the routes from Pattee Ram does not make the above fact less reliable, for whatever inconsistencies there might be regarding relative distances of places, Pattee Ram could hardly make any mistake regarding the position of the boundary. His information agrees with facts already known and any attempt to doubt its credibility would be without foundation.

[3]See Wilson, *Travels of Moorcroft and Trebeck*, 1841, p. 440.

boundary was capable of a general description in terms of mountain ranges and, therefore, less liable to error. Moorcroft says that "on the north Ladakh is bounded by the Pamer or Karakoram mountains." By the Karakoram mountains, he means those ranges which lay both to the west and east of the Karakoram pass, for later on he says: "Eastward from Yarkand, and separated by lofty mountains on the south, a continuation of the Karakoram chain, is the district of Khotan. . . . "

South of Khotan, there are no other "lofty mountains" than those of Kuen Lun and being unaware or unfamiliar with the latter name, he calls it a "continuation of the Karakoram chain." This is the usual mistake which most travellers and geographers made before Johnson's survey. That Moorcroft definitely refers to Kuen Lun is clear also from the description he gives of the Qara Qash and the Yurung Qash rivers. He says that the Qara Qash "rises in the mountains of Khotan, and runs from east to west for twenty-four kos to Shahid Ullah Khajeh." He apparently refers to the course of the Qara Qash from the point it emerges from the Kuen Lun, and he is entirely ignorant of the real source of the Qara Qash further south of the Kuen Lun. He places the source of the Yurang Qash not north-east but "east from the source of the Karakash" in the Haringa Togh (blind mountain).[4]

THE BOUNDARY COMMISSIONS, 1846-47

In regard to the so-called Boundary Commissions of 1846 and 1847, it should be clearly noted that there was agreement on both sides that there already existed an old established boundary and what was required was only the ascertaining of the old boundary. This is clear from the correspondence between the British and Chinese governments. For example, Sir John Davies, the Governor of Hong Kong, in his letter of 18 November 1846 (along with which he forwarded the letter

[4] *Ibid.*, p. 375.

of Lord Hardinge), told Keying, the Chinese viceroy of Canton, that Hardinge's proposal was intended merely "to ascertain the exact boundaries which divide the Thibetan territory from that pertaining to Great Britain, and from that also which has been conferred on Golab Singh." He explained that such a measure would "prevent serious disputes and misunderstandings."[5] The Chinese viceroy evidently mistook the import of the letter and replied on 13 January 1847:

> Respecting the frontiers I beg to state that the borders of those territories have been sufficiently and distinctly fixed so that it will be best to adhere to this ancient arrangement, and it will prove far more convenient to abstain from any additional measures for fixing them.

Davies then explained (21 January 1847) that "it surely was not to offer any new boundaries but merely to ascertain the old ones that Commissioners were sent to Lhassa," and enquired whether the matter had been conveyed to the Chinese Emperor. Keying replied (26 January 1847) that since the British only wished "that the old frontiers may be distinctly known to avoid errors and encroachments," he would convey the wish to the Emperor. Commenting on this reply, Davies wrote to Hardinge that the Chinese had acquiesced "in the propriety of ascertaining the old boundaries, as contradistinguished from fixing any new ones." There is no doubt that this matter had been conveyed to the Chinese Emperor, for, later on, when the British Governor remonstrated on the failure of the Chinese Government to send their deputies to the Ladakh frontier, Keying replied on 7 January 1848 that an Imperial Decree had in fact been issued entrusting the Chinese resident minister in Tibet with the management of the affairs, but that the Decree had not reached him in time.[6]

[5] *Foreign Department, Secret Consultations*, 28 August 1847, 139-183.

[6] *Foreign Department, Secret Consultations*, 31 March 1848, No. 36. The above account would show that Lamb's doubts regarding the reference to Peking, and about Chinese acceptance of the alignment as a delimited one, has no basis in facts.

The 1846 Commission consisting of Cunningham and Vans Agnew returned without visiting the Ladakh frontier, because by the time it completed examination of the boundary between Kashmir and the districts of Lahaul and Spiti, a rebellion had broken out in Kashmir.

The second Commission consisting of Cunningham, Strachey, and Thomson, appointed in 1847, visited the frontier region from the south of Ladakh to the north of Pangong between August 1847 and July 1848 and made detailed enquiries.. The information collected by it was incorporated in Strachey's map of *Nari Khorsum including the easternmost parts of Ladakh with the contiguous districts of Monyul, 1851.*[7] The boundary shown on this map corresponds, with very little difference, to the alignment claimed by India and proves that the Indian alignment has real traditional basis. The areas of Demchok and Western Pangong and the valleys of Chang Chenmo and Changlung Lungpa, which are presently disputed by the Chinese, were clearly shown in India. The Changlung Lungpa valley shown in India included also Khurnak fort which Lamb mistakenly thinks was placed on the boundary line

Dr. Thomson, one of the members of the Commission, travelled up to the Karakoram pass, but could not come to any conclusion regarding the Aksai Chin boundary as he was unable to visit the region. The reference he makes regarding the "unfrequented path" further east evidently applies to the traditional caravan route between Rudok and Khotan via Polu and Keria across the wasteland lying east of Indian Aksai Chin. It was to this route that Deasy was prevented access later in 1898 by the Chinese authorities of Khotan.[8]

The personal opinion of Strachey, cited by Lamb (p. 69), regarding the treaty of 1842, and the objections that the British had on the ground that the treaty gave a monopoly of wool trade to Ladakh, are of little relevance to the problem

[7]This map has been reproduced in the *Atlas of the Northern Frontier of India*, published by the Government of India, 1960, Map 12.

[8]See *Geographical Journal*, Vol. 16, 1900.

for not only is the existence of the treaty now undisputed but it is also recognized that it confirmed the old established boundary.

THE KASHMIR ATLAS

Lamb makes much of the Kashmir Atlas of 1868. The eastern boundary of Ladakh marked on this map is *prima facie* absurd and is certainly not based on the information collected by the surveyors on the ground. Evidence cited by Lamb himself brings out this inconsistency. For example, Godwin Austen, who surveyed the area north of Pangong, considered the valley of the Changlung Lungpa, including the disputed piece of ground around Khurnak, as belonging to Kashmir, while the Kashmir Atlas shows this entire valley outside Kashmir. It would appear, the boundary shown on the Kashmir Atlas as also on some of the sheets of Indian Atlas series blindly copied the eastern boundary of Ladakh from Johnson's sketch map of 1865. This latter map showed the northern boundary of Ladakh correctly along the Kuen Lun, but it was not authoritative for the eastern boundary of Ladakh which was not surveyed by Johnson.

The Kashmir Atlas boundary conflicts also with the first-hand evidence provided by the 1847 Commission. In regard to Demchok, it conflicts with well-established facts of history and with revenue records for the very period that the survey was conducted, which show that Demchok was in the undisputed control of the Kashmir Government.

A critical and unbiased assessment of the evidence available not only in 1864 but as early as 1847 leaves no room for doubt that the alignment claimed by India has firm basis in tradition, custom, and treaties.

6

The Aksai Chin Boundary in 1875: "Mountains constructed in London"

IN DEALING with the northern boundary of Kashmir and Aksai Chin, it is very necessary to bear in mind the manner in which the boundary evolved and the fluctuations it had to undergo as a result of Anglo-Russian rivalry before it crystallized along the Mustagh-Aghil-Kuen Lun line. Here, the limits of the real traditional boundary did not always coincide with the needs of British strategic policies in their various phases, and as Lamb has rightly observed, throughout the British period, the boundary was "distorted this way and that by shifts and changes in the course of British relations with China and Russia." Although the actual course of these "shifts and changes" is too tortuous and complicated to admit of any simplification, it may safely be asserted that the British Government were always willing, in these barren and mountainous areas, to confine themselves to the line which afforded them the best means of defence against a possible Russian presence, or if such Russian designs should ultimately fail to materialize, even to sacrifice their own strategic needs in favour of a "friendly" power such as China if it could effectively occupy and consolidate its position in some of these areas. The traditional territorial rights of Hunza, Kashmir, and Ladakh were of little practical consideration and they were pressed forward or waived strictly in accordance with the needs of the policy stated above. As it happened, since Russian presence in Sinkiang eventually failed to materialize, these rights tended to be waived rather than advanced as a result of British encouragement to China.

It is against this background that the evidence contained in the British records of the nineteenth century should be considered.

Most critics accept Indian title to the Chang Chenmo valley as both valid and proven and there is hardly any need to discuss it further. But in regard to the Aksai Chin area, since some of them prefer to place greater reliance on certain casual opinions expressed by travellers like Hayward and Shaw and on the validity of the so-called MacDonald proposal of 1899, than on the evidence of tradition and Johnson's official survey of 1864, it becomes necessary to examine the relative merits and bases of these sources. And in such an examination, it is scarcely necessary to point out that one has not only to go to the origins of things, but also to view the evidence with care and criticism. When a traveller, for example, says that the Kirghiz frequented the Qara Qash valley, one cannot jump to the conclusion that the entire valley belonged to China, for maybe the reference applied to a particular part of the valley and not to that part which was in dispute; or when a quaint old map shows a so-called Lak Tsung range at a convenient place, one should not, without knowing more about it, try prematurely to find in it an easy solution to a complex international dispute, for such a range may not actually exist on the ground!

THE KUEN LUN IN TRADITION

Alastair Lamb has assumed that Aksai Chin was a sort of no man's land and that nothing definite was known about its ownership until Johnson and the Kashmir authorities arbitrarily extended the boundary of Kashmir to Shahidullah and the Kuen Lun. If this were true and Aksai Chin were really a no man's land the assertion of Kashmir's right through effective occupation would by itself suffice to prove Indian title to the territory. However, the assumption is by no means true. For ages past, there had been an active and flourishing trade between Leh and Yarkand, and the Karakoram route had been traversed by innumerable caravans to and fro. It seems too naive to assume, particularly when even a casual visitor like Hayward could form his own opinion in later times, that these early traders made no enquiries and possessed no knowledge of political frontiers in the region. Evidence of such early knowledge is certainly not lacking. We have seen earlier that Moorcroft referred to the Kuen Lun mountains, the "continuation of the Karakoram chain," as separating the district of Khotan from the territories south of it. This was undoubtedly a reflection of early knowledge of political frontiers and finds abundant corroboration in Chinese works.

Although Chinese works of as early a period as the sixth century A.D. can be cited in this context, it is in the works of the Manchu period that we find precise and almost irrefutable evidence regarding the traditional limits of Sinkiang.[1] Emperor Chien Lung (1735-96), in particular, encouraged historical and geographical research and got several extensive works prepared in which complete knowledge of the huge Chinese empire was collected and which served as the source material for nearly all later descriptions. Thus the *Hsi yu tu chih* of 1762, a geographical work concerning the Western countries (Sinkiang), not only gives a detailed description but illustrates it with a number of extremely interesting maps—both geographical and historical—all of which show specifically that the Nanshan or the Kuen Lun formed the southern boundary of Sinkiang right through history, from the Han to the Ching dynasties. Curiously, in accordance with the state of geographical knowledge of the time (reflected also in Moorcroft's statements cited earlier), it shows the Kuen Lun as a chain in continuation of the Karakoram. It states also that the Khotan (Qara Qash) river rises in the Nanshan mountains showing thereby that the Chinese in 1762 were not even aware of the upper valley of the Qara Qash lying in northern Ladakh (Map 2). Maps and descriptions contained in later works such as *Hsin chiang chi lueh*, compiled at the instance of Emperor Tao Kuang, by a commission of the Peking Academy in

[1]For a list of Chinese works and maps relevant to the problem, see *Report of the Indian Officials*, pp. 45-6.

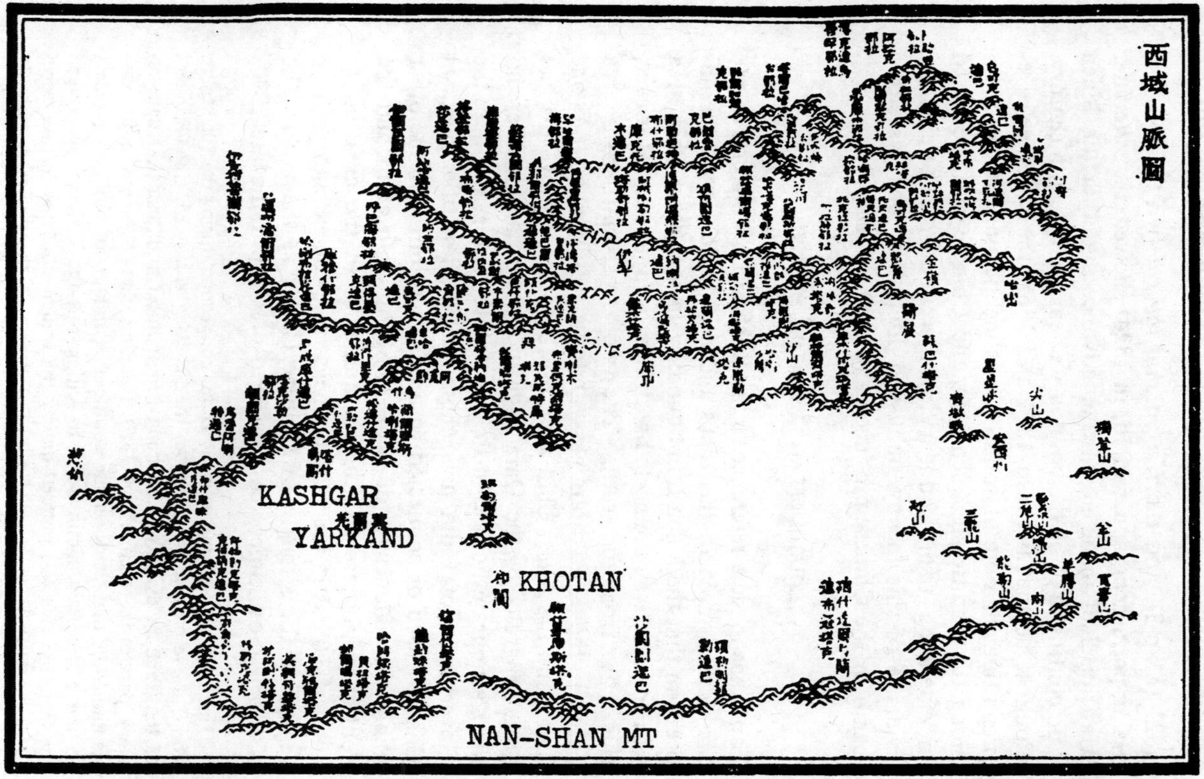

MAP 2. Sinkiang as depicted in *Hsi yu tu chih*, a Chinese work of 1762, which clearly shows Nanshan (Kuen Lun) mountains as the southern boundary

1821 (Map 3), and the *Hsi yu shui tao chi* (written by Hsu Hsing-po, a geographer of Ili, in 1824) showed that the later Manchus had made no further advance and that the Kuen Lun continued to be the boundary in early nineteenth century. Could it be that between 1824 and 1865, the latter year representing the date of Johnson's delineation of the boundary along the traditional Kuen Lun, the Chinese had succeeded in extending their boundary further south? There is no evidence of this in any published literature, nor has either Lamb or the Chinese produced any such evidence.[a]

SHAHIDULLAH AND THE BRITISH

Lamb has made a reference to the Kashmiri occupation of the Shahidullah area in the 1860s and sought to create the impression that the Kuen Lun boundary in the Aksai Chin area was in some way connected with this occupation. However, this is far from the truth. The two areas, that is, the area between the Karakoram pass and Shahidullah, on the one hand, and the Aksai Chin area, on the other, are two distinct areas separated by the Qara Tagh mountains, and neither did the Kashmir authorities in the nineteenth century nor does the Government of India now claim that Indian title to Aksai Chin is based or connected with this question. On the other hand, the significance of both the Shahidullah affair and the continued absence of Chinese authority in the area up to about 1890 lies in the valuable negative evidence they provide regarding the strength of Chinese claims in the area. The Kashmir Government continued to press up to the late 1890s

[a] There was an amusing incident in this connection during the 1960 talks. The Chinese cited a passage from the *Ta ching yi tung chi* (the Gazetteer of the Taching dynasty, containing geographical and historical data on every part of the empire), of 1820, claiming that *Nimangyi* mountains mentioned in that work as the southern boundary of Sinkiang referred to the Karakoram mountains. In citing this the Chinese overlooked the fact, and this was pointed out by the Indian side, that further down in the work, the authors of the Gazetteer had themselves specifically identified *Nimangyi* with the Karangu mountains of the Kuen Lun range!

that they be allowed to reoccupy the Shahidullah area. But neither the British Government nor the Chinese Government were anxious to extend their authority to these barren and rugged areas. For several years the area was left entirely unprotected by either side and appeals by the local people to the Chinese authorities only brought the reply that the areas were not Chinese.[3] This state of affairs had its repercussions on the Ladakh-Yarkand trade and the British Government decided to "induce" the Chinese authorities to occupy the area from Shahidullah to the Karakoram pass. Captain Younghusband was sent to Yarkand and Kashgar for this purpose, and he told the Amban of Yarkand on 5 September 1890:

> His Excellency (the Viceroy of India) had been led to believe that the Chinese considered their frontier extending only as far as the Kilian Pass, and that the intervening country was unoccupied by any power, or, in other words, was a tract of "no man's land." This being an unsatisfactory state of affairs, and one that would afford opportunities for lawless proceedings on the part of the Kanjutis, His Excellency was contemplating extending the Indian frontier to the Kilian Pass, and annex all the country situated between it and the watershed. He had since, however, learned that the Chinese were undertaking the protection of the trade route, and if he found this to be really the case, he would be unwilling to extend the frontier beyond the Karakoram range.[4]

Immediately after this "inducement," the Chinese started showing signs of activity and erected a fort at Suget in the same year and a so-called boundary pillar at the Korakoram pass in September 1892. When the Kashmir Government protested to the British Government against these actions of the Chinese, the latter merely told the former:

[3]See *Report of the Indian Officials*, p. 155.

[4]File Sec. F. March 1891, 123-148, Enclosure to letter dated 19 October 1890 from Resident in Kashmir to Foreign Deptt.

> In principle the Government of India favour the idea of getting the "no man's land" in this locality filled up by the Chinese, subject to future delimitation of boundaries. It does not seem desirable that the responsibilities of the Kashmir State, already heavy, should be increased by the assumption of control over the country beyond the Karakoram.[5]

Thus the question of the boundary in the Karakoram-Shahidullah area was finally decided not so much on the basis of the rights or wrongs of the claims either of the Kashmir or of the Chinese Government as on the basis of the strategic needs of the British Government.

But this decision about the Shahidullah area had nothing to do with the Aksai Chin area about whose status no discussion took place in this connection.

THE AKSAI CHIN BOUNDARY

Lamb recognizes that the new trade routes opened by the Indian authorities in late 1860s "started in the region of the Chang Chenmo valley and then crossed to wastes of the Aksai Chin area till they came to upper reaches of the Karakash river"; but from the boundary point of view, he thinks, that although the Karakoram pass had been recognized as the boundary in Moorcroft's day and in the time of the 1846 and 1847 boundary commissions, the newly started trade activity provided a pretext for British officials to see as "red on the map" all the country traversed by the new trade routes up to the now "effective Kashmir-Yakub Bey Boundary post" near Shahidullah. In putting the matter this way, Lamb has mixed up a number of unrelated issues. As stated earlier, the Shahidullah-Karakoram area is distinct from the Aksai Chin area and has an altogether different background. The fluctuations of the effective border in the Shahidullah area towards Karakoram had no influence whatsoever on the traditional boundary in the

[5]File S.F. January 1893, No. 508.

Aksai Chin area. What Moorcroft and the Boundary Commission of 1847 stated about the Karakoram pass did not affect the status of Aksai Chin. Indeed, Moorcroft had different things to say about these two different areas. Similarly, whatever reasons the British officials had to see as "red on the map" in the Shahidullah-Karakoram and Shahidullah-Kuen Lun sections, they had no application to the Aksai Chin section which lay further east and south respectively of the two sections, and where both tradition and practice consistently pointed towards the Kuen Lun as the boundary.

Johnson, at the time of his survey of Aksai Chin, was not an employee of the Kashmir Government. He had been specifically assigned by the Survey of India to survey the Aksai Chin area in 1865, and he did it with great ability. Although due to the pioneering nature of the work certain technical errors had crept in, these were duly corrected before the publication of the map. The genuineness of the boundary marked by him was never doubted, for it fully accorded with the actual state of occupation which happened to correspond with the traditional boundary in the Kuen Lun area and the effective border in the Shahidullah area.[6] There is no evidence whatsoever for ascribing his boundary delineation to political motives. Johnson's crossing of the Kuen Lun boundary at the invitation of the Ruler of Khotan, his subsequent resignation from the Survey of India and appointment with the Kashmir Durbar have no relevance at all with his survey work and boundary delineation in the Aksai Chin area. Indeed, far from finding fault with Johnson's work, the official report of the Survey of India for 1865 spoke of Johnson's work in the following terms:

> Mr. Johnson's explorations this season completed a most valuable and important work. Throughout the expedition to Khotan and the adjacent countries, he displayed great energy and perseverance to accomplish what he did; and

[6]For extracts from his report, see *Report of the Indian Officials*, pp. 144-5

every credit is due to him for being the first to give any account of these previously unknown regions. In 1875 a gold watch was presented by the Royal Geographical Society to Mr. Johnson in acknowledgement of the services rendered to geography by his survey journey in 1865 across the Kuen Luen to Ilchi, and "for the aid subsequently rendered to Sir D. Forsyth's expedition, whilst resident at Ladakh."[7]

The northern boundary of Kashmir as marked by Johnson came to be revised in later years due to the shifts in British policy in regard to the Shahidullah section. But the basis of the boundary he marked along the Kuen Lun in the Aksai Chin section remained unchallenged by authoritative circles. Dr. Henderson who accompanied the Forsyth Mission in 1870 considered Aksai Chin as a no man's land, but not as Chinese. R.B. Shaw objected to the inclusion of Shahidullah in Kashmir territory, but as to the southern limits of Khotan further east, he had no doubt that the Kuen Lun formed the boundary. In a paper he read before the Royal Geographical Society in 1871 he stated: "Eastern Turkistan (or as it used to be called on our maps, Chinese Tartary) resembles a huge bay, with its mouth turned to the east, and shut in on every other side by gigantic chains of mountains." He then proceeded to describe the formation of the Thian-Shan and the Kuen Lun ranges forming the northern and southern ramparts of Sinkiang.[8]

G.W. Hayward also objected to the inclusion of the Shahidullah area, mainly on the ground that "the valleys of the Yarkand and Karakash rivers are frequented by the Kirghiz who all pay tribute to the ruler of Turkistan." There is no doubt that by the Qara Qash valley he meant the lower Qara Qash valley lying to the north of Aksai Chin, for the upper Qara Qash was frequented more by Ladakhis than by the Kirghiz. As for the so-called natural boundary that Hayward

[7] *Report of the Great Trigonometrical Survey, Synoptical Volume VII*, 1879, p. XLII.

[8] *Proceedings of the RGS*, Vol. XIV, pp. 125-6.

laid down along the main line of the Karakoram up to the Chang Chenmo passes, there is neither geographical nor historical basis. A study of the map attached to his article shows how greatly mistaken he was regarding the geography of the region. He traces a continuous line of mountains, evidently his "main Karakoram range," running east and south from the Karakoram pass and skirting the Shyok and the Chang Chenmo basins on the eastern side. Later surveys revealed that the main Karakoram range lay far west between the two bends of the Shyok, and that east of the latter river there was but a tangled mass of mountains running in all directions and providing no convenient and simple formula for a "natural boundary."

The boundary which Trelawney Saunders marked on his map of June 1873 was no other than the "natural boundary" described by Hayward, and has an interesting history behind it. It so happened that Hayward's map, shortly after its publication, was sent by Douglas Forsyth to the Survey of India with instructions to the effect that the details of features shown on the map should be incorporated in the Survey of India's map of *Turkestan*. This was, of course, nothing unusual because survey maps are constantly revised on the basis of new explorations and surveys. However, in the process, Forsyth overlooked the fact that Hayward had drawn a thin dotted line along the chain of mountains, the "natural boundary," which he thought existed east of the Shyok river. The Survey of India "fitted" both the features and the "boundary," though with considerable difficulty, on the *Turkestan* map. Several copies of this map were sent to London, and apparently Trelawney Saunders copied his features and the boundary from this map or from Hayward's map direct. The error regarding the boundary was soon discovered in Simla, and the Government of India declared the map "unauthoritative" and decided that the boundary was not to be delineated "without communicating to Maharaja of Cashmere."[9]

[9] *Foreign Department Pol.* A. July 1873, 452-453; and *Pol.* A. September 1873, 304-308.

Forsyth was thereafter inclined to be careful regarding boundary matters, and in the official report he submitted to the government regarding his mission to Kashgar, in 1873-74, he not only stated that the boundary lay at Yangi Dawan on the Kuen Lun but traced in his map a boundary which was in some respects more forward than that of Johnson. This was traced evidently on the principle of the "effective border" and if he expressed any doubts when he used the words "approximate" and "not authoritative" he only meant that the British Government might not agree to defend this border all along and that they might change it by a few miles this or that way (perhaps in the Shahidullah area). Trotter, the official surveyor, who accompanied Forsyth, it should be noted, clearly stated: "As Shahidullah was the first point when we struck the Atalik's dominions and *met his peoples*, I briefly give the result of survey operations up to that point."[10]

The general impression to be derived from the various sources which have been quoted above is that as in the days of Moorcroft and the Chinese works of the eighteenth and early nineteenth centuries, no serious doubts were ever entertained regarding the traditional boundary along the Kuen Lun. Novel ideas regarding a so-called natural boundary were confined to a few individuals like Hayward and Saunders who apparently did not have sufficient information regarding the precise alignment of mountains in the region. Indeed, precisely in the 1870s a fierce controversy was going on among geographers regarding these very features[11] and, as one of the later geographers has remarked, Trelawney Saunders was often found to be speaking on the basis of "mountains that had been constructed in London." If in 1875, therefore, there was a boundary other than the Kuen Lun boundary it was the one based on the "mountains that had been constructed in London."

[10]Forsyth, *Report of a Mission to Yarkand in 1873*, p. 283.
[11]See JRGS 1872 and *Geographical Journals*, 1877 and 1878.

7

Kashmir-Sinkiang Boundary Before 1947

THE HUNZA FRONTIER provides a better example than that of Shahidullah regarding the manner in which the British Government tended to subordinate the rights of Kashmir to the needs of policy and strategy. Adjoining Hunza in the north-east is the valley of the Raskam river extending from the Taghdumbash Pamir in the west to the Karakoram pass in the east. It is bounded on the north by the Kuen Lun mountains and on the south by the Mustagh and the Aghil-Karakorams. Younghusband, who visited the region in 1889, described it thus:

> The whole of this tract is a vast mass of lofty mountains, and even the lowest valley-bottoms are situated at a very considerable altitude above the sea-level. With the exception of a few Kirghiz on the Taghdumbash Pamir and at Shahidula, it is entirely unpopulated, and, owing to its extreme elevation and the rigour of the climate, is, except in a few places along the Yarkand River, uncultivable. The mountain summits are covered with perpetual snow, and their sides—sometimes rocky precipices and sometimes steep slopes of shale and debris—are always utterly devoid of vegetation; so that in the whole of this tract not a single tree is to be seen on the mountain-sides, and even in the valley bottoms only in a few places in the lowest part of Raskam.[1]

It is generally assumed that this area became a part of the Chinese empire when Emperor Chien Lung conquered Turkestan. But there has seldom been any attempt made to examine

[1]F.E. Younghusband, *Report of a Mission to the Northern Frontier of India*, p. 91.

whether this assumption has any basis in history. Chinese works like the *Hsi yu tu chih*, written in Chien Lung's time, contain only vague references to the source of the Yarkand in the Tsungling mountains. But the maps attached to the work show that they were aware only of the lower course of the Yarkand river from the point where it emerged from the Kuen Lun mountains and that they were not aware of the courses of the upper tributaries of Raskam and Shaksgam rivers nor of the Karakoram mountains lying further south. Indeed the maps show only one line of mountains, namely, the Kuen Lun, skirting Sinkiang in the south-west. There is no evidence of the Chinese ever having exercised any jurisdiction in the Raskam valley before the 1890s. On the other hand, there is positive evidence to show that the Chinese at that time considered the Kuen Lun as their southern boundary. During 1879-80, for example, Ney Elias who travelled in the region was told by the Chinese that "they considered their line of 'chatze' or posts as their frontier—viz. Kugiar, Kilian, Sanju, Kiria, etc., and that they had no concern with what lay beyond the mountains (the Kuen Lun)." Subsequent travellers, including Younghusband in 1889, collected evidence to similar effect, and in his official report submitted to the Government in 1890 Younghusband observed:

> ... the Chinese have never asserted an authority over the valley of the Yarkand River, and it is only this year that they have asserted any definite authority over the Shahidula district, the limits of their jurisdiction for all practical purposes having hitherto been the Kuen Lun range, with frontier posts at Kugiar, Kilian, and Sanju. In their former occupation of Turkestan the Chinese certainly made no pretensions to any authority on the southern side of the Kuen Lun Mountains.[2]

[2] *Ibid.*, pp. 99-100. The Raskam was often referred to in the early days as the Yarkand river. The latter name is now applied only to the section lying north of the junction between the Raskam and the Shaksgam.

SO-CALLED CHINESE SUZERAINTY

As in the case of the Raskam valley, the so-called Chinese claims on Hunza have also seldom been critically examined. Although the early history of Hunza is obscure there yet is no evidence whatsoever of any Chinese influence. Unlike the Kirghiz of the north the Hunza people are of Iranian and Turanian origin and their relations were always with the people of the south and the west. The Chinese claimed that Hunza became a tributary of the Chinese empire in the twenty-fifth year of the reign of Chien Lung (A.D. 1760). But there is no record of Hunza ever having been invaded by the Chinese troops. Indeed, according to the Hunza version, it was the Mir of Hunza who invaded and defeated the Kirghiz nomads of the Taghdumbash Pamir and informed the Chinese that Hunza territory thenceforth extended up to Dafdar in the Taghdumbash. The Chinese made a present to the Mir for having conquered their enemies and the Mir acknowledged it by a small gift of gold dust[3] which was no more a tribute than what Macartney offered to the Emperor of the "Middle Kingdom" in 1793. The exchange of presents became an annual feature and it is only in later years that the Chinese, encouraged by the reluctance of the British to accept responsibility for the trans-Mustagh region and their anxiety to see Chinese power effectively asserted there, distorted it as a tributary relationship and made it a basis for a territorial claim. The northern limits of the territories conquered by the Mir of Hunza were:

> The northern watershed of the Tagdumbash Pamir from the Wakhirjui pass through the Beyik peak to Ilijilga about a mile above Dafdar, thence across the river to the Zankan nullah: thence through Mazar and over the range to Urok a point on the Yarkand river between Sibjaida and Itakturuk. Thence it runs along the northern watershed of the

[3]S.F. July 1898, No. 327.
[4]S.F. July 1898, No. 327, para 12.

Raskam valley to the junction of the Bazar Dara river and the Yarkand river. From thence southwards over the mountains to the Mustagh river leaving Aghil Dawan and Aghil pass within Hunza limits.

Before the 1890s there is no evidence to show that Hunza was either considered a vassal or acted as a vassal of China. Moorcroft travelling in 1821 noted that Hunza was an "independent" State.[5] Hunza's rights over the Taghdumbash and Raskam areas were regularly exercised by the Mir except during the short period between 1865 and 1878 when Yakub Beg ruled in Turkestan. In about 1885, when the Sarikulis of Tashkurgan declined to pay revenue to Hunza, the Taotai of Kashgar intervened and ruled that Hunza rights extended over the Taghdumbash and the Khunjerab Pamirs up to Dafdar. An agreement was also drawn up laying down the northern limits of Hunza.[6] The Mir continued to collect the revenue himself until 1896 whereafter the Taotai undertook to do it on the Mir's behalf.

While thus the authority of the Mir of Hunza over the Taghdumbash and Raskam areas had received definite recognition, and the Chinese claim of jurisdiction over these areas and Hunza was based only on the flimsy pretext of an exchange of presents and therefore always remained shadowy, the authority of Kashmir over Hunza came to be established without the least doubt by 1869. Gilgit had been conquered by the Sikh rulers of Kashmir as early as 1842, that is, some four years prior to the extension of British authority over Kashmir, and attempts made simultaneously to subdue Hunza. But in 1869 the Mir of Hunza recognized the authority of the Ruler of Kashmir and started paying tribute. In 1891 the British authorities intervened only to assist Kashmir to put down the revolt of Hunza and to re-establish Kashmir authority.

[5]Wilson, *Travels of Moorcroft and Trebeek*, Vol. II, p. 261.
[6]S.F. July 1898, No. 327, para 13.

RUSSOPHOBIA

By the year 1890 the prospect of a Russian advance into Sinkiang had become very real. The previous three decades had already seen a rapid advance and consolidation of its power in the whole of western Turkestan including the Khanates of Khiva, Bokhara, and Khokand, and its attention had now been directed towards an advance in the Pamir region. British plans against such Russian advance had, after a great deal of controversy and after the experience of the two Afghan wars, settled down in favour of a strategically sound frontier buttressed by a politically safe buffer. Steps were taken to secure a strong Indo-Afghan frontier along a line commanding the strategic passes and to ensure the stability and loyalty of the Afghan regime through various measures. Afghanistan's frontier with Russia in the western sector was defined and demarcated between 1873 and 1887.

When the Russian threat developed on the Pamirs, the first reaction of the British Government was in terms of another buffer region. China was not yet in a position to threaten the British possessions in India and a strategic frontier in the north had reference, for the time being, mainly to the Pamir regions. Here both China and Afghanistan were to be persuaded to close up their ranks and to create an effective buffer which would set a limit to the Russian advance. Thus Ney Elias who was deputed in 1885 to Chinese Turkestan and to Badakshan "to watch the movements of the Russians in and around the regions" drew attention to the threat that a Russian occupation of the Pamirs would mean to the "passes leading into Chitral" and recommended:

> It is precisely this fulfilment of a Russian desire that I believe can be frustrated (as long as Afghanistan and China remain outwardly friendly to England) by closing up Afghan and Chinese territory to a common frontier line across the belt in question, and leaving to Russia only the possibility of violating it by an open act of aggression or war.

During 1889-90, the Government of India deputed another officer, F.E. Younghusband, on the basis of whose reports they recommended to the Secretary of State for India in July 1890:

> We are of opinion that we should no longer delay taking some steps towards closing this gap.... We think that the end we have in view, viz. the effectual establishment of Chinese authority over the country up to the limits of Afghan territory, might be facilitated by frankly explaining the situation to the Chinese Government. We should, therefore, ask that it should be addressed on the subject by Her Majesty's Government.... We would further wish the Chinese Government to be informed that we desire to see the frontiers of Chinese Turkistan coterminous with those of Afghanistan and Kashmir and its dependencies.[7]

Later in March 1891 the Government of India sent a concrete proposal suggesting the definition of a boundary between China and Afghanistan along a line which would leave the whole of the Alichur Pamirs (now part of Afghanistan and the USSR) in China.[8] The British Government formally asked the Chinese Government whether such a boundary would be acceptable to them.[9]

It is in this context of setting a limit to the Russian advance and of establishing a Chinese buffer that the British Government gave incidental consideration to the relative claims of China and Kashmir to the territories lying between the Karakoram and the Kuen Lun; and where the Government of Kashmir or of an independent India would have tended to subordinate considerations of strategy to those of prestige and genuine claims, the British Government tended to subordinate claims to strategy. Thus, right from the beginning

[7]S.F. July 1890, No. 243.
[8]S.F. March 1891, No. 147.
[9]S.F. August 1891, Nos. 112-115.

the British Government thought not in terms of occupying a territory which was lying defenceless and unclaimed by the Chinese, and over which Hunza and Kashmir had genuine claims, but in terms of limiting their own responsibilities and securing a strategically sound and politically safe frontier.

Thus Ney Elias, who had earlier reported the absence of any Chinese jurisdiction in the upper Yarkand valley, presented the political and strategic aspect involved in the occupation of the valley in the following terms:

> Supposing it is decided to take in the "no man's land," we should have to open regular negotiations with China (the most impracticable nation), and have a formal Delimitation Commission to determine an artificial frontier line. If satisfactorily completed, some portions of it would be uninhabited, or, at all events, inhabitable country, at easy altitudes, readily accessible from the north, but cut off from our side by the heights of the Indus waterparting ranges, the passes over which are only practicable for about seven months in the year. At certain points (as on the Yarkand and Karakash rivers), this frontier would have to be guarded by outposts of Kashmiri troops which would be cut off from their base, in Ladak, for some five months of each year; while for the remainder of the year it would be difficult to support and supply them.

He recommended, as the "simplest solution" of the matter, that the Chinese be induced to occupy the entire territory involved and that "a preliminary step towards such a solution would, for the present, be to acknowledge the Chinese nationality of the Karakash Kirghiz, and to encourage them to reoccupy the section of the Yarkand river valley...."[10]

Lord Lansdowne, the Viceroy, agreed with the above view and ruled:

[10]S.F. October 1889, Nos. 182-197, Notes K.W.2.

The country between the Karakorum and Kuen Lun ranges, is, I understand, of no value, very inaccessible and not likely to be coveted by Russia. We might, I should think, encourage the Chinese to take it, if they showed any inclination to do so. This would be better than leaving a no man's land between our frontier and that of China. Moreover the stronger we can make China at this point, and the more we can induce her to hold her own over the whole Kashgar-Yarkand region, the more useful will she be to us as an obstacle to Russian advance along this line.[11]

CHINESE FORWARD POLICY

It is in fulfilment of the above policy that Captain Younghusband was deputed in 1889 and 1890 to Yarkand and Kashgar and, as has been noted in connection with the Shahidullah boundary, the Chinese immediately started taking interest in the region. Besides setting up a "pillar" at the Karakoram pass, they formally raised, for the first time, the question of Hunza's so-called vassalage to China. This they did evidently at the instance of the deposed Chief of Hunza who had taken refuge in Yarkand. The British Government were reluctant to take any decisive action on this question because the so-called tribute paid by Hunza had now become inextricably involved with the rights that the chief exercised in Taghdumbash and in the Raskam valley. A stoppage of the "tribute" at this stage would result in his losing his rights in these areas which might eventually be occupied by the Russians. In order to prevent this possibility it was necessary to keep both the "tribute" and the Mir's rights alive until the Chinese were in a position effectively to assert their authority in the Taghdumbash region. The best course, therefore, appeared to be to allow matters to drift. The government ruled:

If China will hold the Taghdumbash Pamir effectively, the Government of India will certainly *not be disposed*, under

[11]S.F. October 1889, Nos. 182-197, p. 4/n.

present conditions, to *press that claim* against her. But it may be desirable that, without being pressed, the claim should be kept alive. The Russians have shown some interest in the Taghdumbash Pamir, and if China retired from it, they would doubtless occupy it.[12]

The Chinese were now feeling encouraged to become more assertive and to claim, as a matter of right, territories which they had scarcely bothered to occupy and administer earlier and which the British themselves had asked them to occupy. They started increasingly to interfere with the rights which the Chief of Hunza had been exercising in the Taghdumbash and Raskam and to displace the people of Hunza with the Kirghiz and the Sarikolis. They were encouraged in this by the Russians who, like the British, were equally anxious now to preserve this region as a buffer zone. In 1895 information was received to the effect that the Chinese had started patrolling the Taghdumbash area.[13]

In 1895 Major Gerard, who had been deputed to demarcate the Russo-Afghan boundary, asked for clear instructions regarding the status of Taghdumbash, as the matter was likely to crop up during the demarcation work. But the British Government, who were closely watching the gradual assertion of Chinese authority and considered such assertion as a "welcome step" and a "matter for congratulation," were still uncertain whether such assertion of authority was effective enough against a Russian advance. Until they were so satisfied they proposed to keep Hunza's claims in theory. The Secretary of State wired:

> ...We consider that Taghdumbash Pamir is subject to concurrent rights of China and Kanjut. We do not propose to make any claim, however, on account of latter except for the purpose of precaution against China ceding it to Russia....[14]

[12]S.E. December 1892, 136-148.
[13]S.F. October 1895, Nos. 150-173, K.W.No. 2.
[14]S.F. October 1895, No. 168.

MACARTNEY

This policy of adhesion to Hunza's claims in theory and their relinquishment in practice had its attendant dangers. Officials, like Macartney, believed that Russia's occupation of Kashgar was imminent and in that eventuality claims which had been surrendered in practice would be difficult to revive. After all, the claims of Kashmir were not mere pretentions (as Lamb makes out to be—p. 100—through a misinterpretation of Macartney's despatch). Macartney, therefore, suggested that the Government of India should enter into a treaty with China making the cession of Taghdumbash conditional on her ability to retain control in the area.[15] Macartney also foresaw the possibility of creating an independent neutral State between the Karakoram and the Kuen Lun. In September 1895 news was received that the demarcation of the Russo-Afghan boundary had been completed and that the Russians had given an assurance that the watershed of the Taghdumbash along the Sarikol would be considered as the Sino-Soviet boundary. Nevertheless, the Government of India was not prepared to trust such assurances, and on the suggestion of Macartney, referred to above, proposed to the Secretary of State that steps might be taken to enter into an agreement with China regarding a frontier settlement which should safeguard Kashmir's rights over the Taghdumbash.

ARDAGH AND THE BOUNDARY

The British Foreign Office replied that before an approach was made to the Chinese Government on the subject it was desirable "to acquire an efficient control within the frontiers that may be considered as falling within the legitimate range of British influence" and asked the Government of India to put forth its own views. The Foreign Office also forwarded a note prepared by Sir John Ardagh, Director of the Intelli-

[15]S.F. October 1895, No. 157.

gence Division of the War Office, suggesting three alternative lines. Ardagh questioned the strategic basis of the Mustagh-Karakoram boundary and proposed that

> we should aim at keeping our enemy from any possibility of establishing himself on the glacis, occupying these longitudinal valleys, and there preparing to surprise the passes. We should, therefore, seek a boundary which shall leave all these longitudinal valleys in our possession, or at least under our influence.

The lines suggested by him were along the Kuen Lun, the Yarkand river and a third line further south.[16] Sir John Ardagh considered these lines politically justifiable as the Kashmir Government had legitimate claims over them; and the Foreign Office apparently agreed with this view when they referred, in their forwarding letter, to the "legitimate range of British influence."

These alignments suggested by Sir John Ardagh were not far different from one of the alignments which Younghusband had also suggested as early as 1890. He had thought of a boundary which would run

> along the spur from the Kuen Lun range which is crossed by the Suget and Sokh-bulak Passes, and would continue along the crest of the Kuen Lun Mountains to their western extremity, and then, crossing the Yarkand River below the junction of the Ilisu, strike the Kurbu range near the Kurbu Pass, and run along it till it met the Mustagh Mountains east of the Khuenjerab Pass.[17]

[16]S.F. January 1898, No. 166.

[17]Younghusband, *Report of a Mission to the Northern Frontier of Kashmir*, p. 100. Younghusband had also suggested an alternative boundary running along the Mustagh, the Karakoram, the Qara Tagh, and the Kuen Lun. But this was only on the assumption that the British Government was opposed to the Kuen Lun boundary on grounds of policy and strategy.

Nor were they very different from the boundary which Hung Ta-chin, late Chinese Minister to the court of St. Petersburg, showed on his maps (see Maps 4 and 5). These maps had been drawn before 1890—the date from which the Chinese, encouraged by British inducements, had launched on a forward policy—and represented the actual state of affairs regarding the boundaries.[18]

ELGIN-CUNNINGHAM BOUNDARY: MACDONALD PROPOSAL

The Government of India, then headed by Lord Elgin, were disinclined to agree with the boundaries suggested by Sir John Ardagh, both on political and military grounds. They argued, rather curiously, that "the Chinese have, on more than one occasion, evinced a determination to assert their territorial rights in the direction of the Indian frontier" and that "any attempt to incorporate within our frontier either of the zones mentioned by Sir John Ardagh would involve real risk of strained relations with China and might tend to precipitate the active interposition of Russia in Kashgaria, which it should be our aim to postpone as long as possible." From the military point of view they saw "no strategic advantage in going beyond mountains over which no hostile advance is ever likely to be attempted.... No invader has ever approached India from this direction where nature has placed such formidable barriers."[19]

In October the same year the Government of India formulated their own proposal which was ultimately conveyed to the Government of China by Sir Claude MacDonald on 14 March 1899. This proposal included in Indian territory none of the

[18]See S.F. August 1893, No. 342; and S.F. October 1893, No. 97. The maps were a part of a series of 35 sheets and contrary to what Lamb has suggested (p. 101 and Appendix) there is evidence to show that the Kashmir-Sinkiang boundary shown therein represented the official view of the Chinese Government at the time. Almost all earlier maps showed alignments somewhat similar to this.

[19]S.F. January 1898, No. 168.

areas lying north of the Mustagh-Karakoram which Sir John Ardagh had thought justifiable to claim, except a small insignificant portion in the Taghdumbash area. In return for the relinquishment by China of "her shadowy claim to suzerainty over the State of Kanjut," it offered to relinquish Hunza's claims to a major part of the Taghdumbash and the whole of Raskam district. In the Aksai Chin area it proposed a boundary along the so-called Lak Tsung range up to a spur running south from the Kuen Lun range at a point east of 80° East Longitude.

The manner in which the proposal was put forward, and the nature of discussions which preceded it, show to what extent Elgin's administration had become a victim of its own deception in regard to the political and military aspects of the frontier in the Hunza area and how little consideration it gave to the question of the Aksai Chin boundary. Although right from the beginning discussions on the frontier question had been inhibited by the policy decisions already taken in the early 1890s, Elgin's administration had gone so far as to forget that if the exchange of presents between the Mir of Hunza and the Chinese Government had been allowed to continue, it was not because the Government was at any time prepared to admit the fictitious claims of Chinese suzerainty over Hunza, but because of policy considerations which were entirely extraneous to such claims. In equating the territorial rights of Hunza with the shadowy claims of China over Hunza, therefore, the Government of India were committing a grave error which met with severe opposition both from the Mir of Hunza and well-informed officials like Sir A. Talbot, Resident in Kashmir, and Captain McMahon who was then Political Agent in Gilgit. McMahon put forward strong arguments based on a detailed appreciation of the origin and history of the relative claims of Hunza and China to show that, while the Chinese claims on Hunza were purely nominal and their claims on the territory south of the Kuen Lun had not been backed by actual exercise of administration, the rights of Hunza to the Taghdumbash, Khunjerab, and Raskam areas had, both on theoretical and practical grounds, been "proved beyond doubt." As for the political and military aspects involved, he thought:

> ... however strong the arguments may appear at first sight for restricting ourselves to a definite frontier like the Hindu Kush and Mustagh ranges on strategic grounds, it would be wise, I venture to think, before irrevocably committing ourselves to such a frontier, to carefully consider the wisdom of gratuitously surrendering, in doing so, territory which belongs to the people on whom we will have to depend for active assistance in defending that frontier.

Sir A. Talbot agreed with McMahon's view and recommended that "we ought to do all in our power to secure for Hunza, lands to which she seems to have a fair claim." He said:

> There can be little doubt that Hunza vassalage to China, if such it can be called, was purely nominal, and the Kirghiz tribes who inhabited the Pamir countries between Kashgar and Yarkand and the Kilik and Mintaka passes were, until recent years, entirely independent of Chinese control.[20]

On the military aspects of the question, Captain Deasy, who had travelled extensively in the region, noted: "Raskam could easily be defended if the boundaries suggested by me are agreed upon, as the nature of the country renders it quite needless to employ a large garrison at either end and no troops are required elsewhere."[21] However, the British Government, influenced largely by the fear of Russian intervention and on the advice of their own military experts, decided to ignore the legitimate rights of Hunza and favoured a boundary along the Mustagh.

[20]S.F. July 1898, No. 326 and Enclosures.
[21]S.F. August 1899, No. 175.

LAK TSUNG RANGE: "MOUNTAINS CONSTRUCTED IN LONDON"

As for the Aksai Chin area, the matter was then of so little importance—politically and militarily—and British officials had so little knowledge of the relative claims of Kashmir and Sinkiang that it received little or no consideration at the time of the British Government's proposal of 1898-99. Earlier, in 1893, Macartney had noted that Hung Ta-chin's map had shown Aksai Chin in India. Later, in October 1896, the Taotai of Kashgar, at the instigation of the Russian Consul, complained that Aksai Chin which belonged to "Chinese Tibet" had wrongly been included in British territory in one of the British atlases. The Taotai had apparently little knowledge either of the geography or of the precise political status of Aksai Chin, for he claimed it as a part of "Chinese Tibet," little anticipating that the Chinese Government would later claim it as part of Chinese Sinkiang. Macartney pointed out that Aksai Chin was a vast area and that it was partly in Chinese and partly in British territory.[22]

In July 1898, in connection with the proposal to be sent to London, the Foreign Secretary, W.J. Cunningham, got a line marked by Younghusband along the crest of the Mustagh and Karakoram (except in the Darwaza area) up to 76° E Longitude on the map of *Northern Trans-Frontier*, and asked the Surveyor General to transfer the line to a larger map which included the eastern portion as well. He instructed that the line should be continued along the crest of the mountains up to the Karakoram pass and thereafter "so far as the boun-

[22]S.F. January 1898, No. 162. Macartney was evidently referring to the western and eastern parts of Aksai Chin, the eastern one being Chinese. He made no suggestions regarding a boundary line along the Lak Tsung range or regarding any division of Aksai Chin into northern and southern parts. The reference which Lamb gives in this connection, namely, Elgin's letter to Hamilton dated 23 December 1897, mentions Taotai's complaint regarding Aksai Chin, but makes no allusion to any suggestion by Macartney. Macartney had earlier (1895) sent a note regarding the creation of a neutral State but this had no reference to the Aksai Chin boundary.

dary is that between Kashmir and Khotan." No precise instructions were given about the features to be followed east of the Karakoram pass. The Surveyor General marked the boundary on a map illustrating Younghusband's explorations (16-mile scale) up to 79° E Longitude. He expressed inability to mark the further portion as the map did not extend beyond that point. There was no suitable map on which this portion could be marked. The Foreign Secretary then found among his old papers a map prepared by Trotter in 1874 on which a so-called Lak Tsung range had been superimposed in red ink in a prominent manner. The Foreign Secretary noted that this range "would seem to show a good line from 79° E, a little north of 35° N . . . to meet the spur running south from the Kuen Lun range which on our maps forms the boundary between China and Kashmir." Thereafter he proceeded to draft the description of the boundary which he despatched to London and was eventually submitted by MacDonald to the Tsungli Yamen.[23]

Thus the description of the boundary along the "Lak Tsung range" came to be inserted very casually in the despatch without any discussion or consideration whatsoever, and neither the so-called moderate nor the so-called forward schools had anything to do with it. Macartney had certainly nothing to do with it and, as later surveys have shown, there is no such thing as a "Lak Tsung range" (see Maps 1 and 5). Cunningham's successors wondered "what on earth induced Sir W. Cunningham to recommend this boundary. . . ."[24]

MODERATE AND FORWARD

The application of the terms "moderate" and "forward" in relation to the Kashmir-Sinkiang boundary is highly misleading and is based on a wrong understanding of the problem. Unlike the Indo-Afghan boundary where the British forward

[23]S.F. November 1898, 110-114/notes.

[24]S.F. February 1908, Nos. 40-51, L.W. Dane's note dated 18 October 1907.

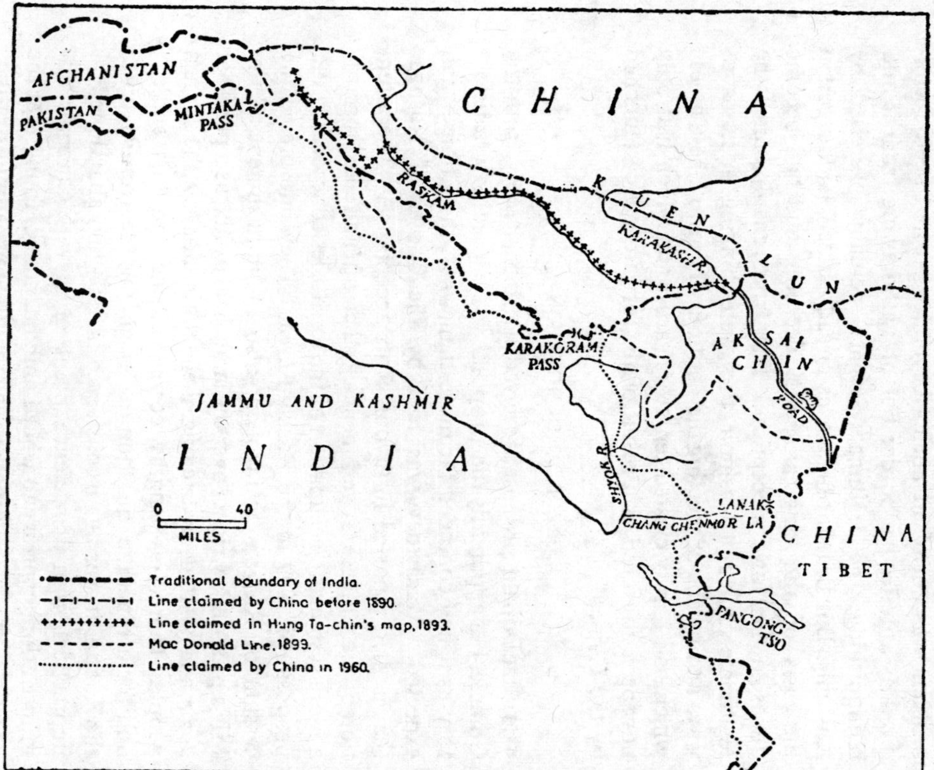

MAP 5. Northern Kashmir

school had often toyed with the idea of advancing British control up to the Hindu Kush, on the Kashmir boundary the problem was not of advancing beyond what had been recognized as an effective border but of withdrawing from it and relinquishing the legitimate rights actually exercised by Kashmir. But British officials, as already stated, had forgotten the basis of the original policy decisions and had become dupes to their own deception. Far from championing the legitimate claims of Kashmir, they were thinking in terms of ways and means of meeting the fictitious claims of the Chinese which had hardly existed ten years earlier and which had only now been advanced as a result of the forward policy launched by the Chinese.

CURZON AND MCMAHON

The MacDonald proposal received no formal reply from the Chinese, but apparently the proposal was exceedingly satisfactory as it had conceded far more than what the Chinese had expected. Macartney was told by the Taotai of Kashgar that he had reported in favour of its acceptance. The attention of the Chinese Government was thereafter directed towards a more systematic occupation of the territories conceded by the proposal of 1899 in the Raskam area. They interpreted the cession of Raskam as involving also a relinquishment of the Mir's proprietary rights over the lands held by him as a personal *Jagir* and started obstructing their cultivation by the Hunza people. There was lengthy correspondence on this subject, and for a time the question of extending the frontier up to the Kuen Lun was again considered in 1904 and abandoned as impractical from the defence point of view.[25] Curzon's administration, contrary to what Lamb has stated, found that the practical effect of the policies of the previous administrations had reached such a pass that it would be impossible to assert the Mir's rights in the Raskam valley without using force. Curzon's government was, therefore, inclined to accept a boundary settlement provided the previous proposal was

[25]S.E. February 1905, 1398-1445, p. 3/n.

modified in the Shaksgam valley area where the jurisdiction of the Mir was still respected by the Chinese.

After the Chinese revolution of 1911, the outbreak of disturbances in Sinkiang and renewed fears of Russian occupation of Kashgar revived the question of the Kashmir-Sinkiang boundary, and the Government of India gave fresh consideration to it. This time McMahon, who had now become Foreign Secretary, had no hesitation in upholding the rights of Hunza and suggesting a boundary along the line proposed by Sir John Ardagh. The General Staff which had previously opposed the line now modified its view to state that "the extended frontier would be an advantage provided we have not to occupy the portion beyond our present frontier by posts, but merely aim at keeping it undeveloped."[26]

The Government of India then wrote to London to state that, although they did not favour any diplomatic moves which would facilitate Russian occupation of Sinkiang, if such an occupation was forced on them, they would urge the recognition by Russia of a boundary which would leave the Taghdumbash, Raskam, Shahidullah, and Aksai Chin within India. The British Government, accordingly, initiated negotiations with the Russian Government but reached no settlement owing to the outbreak of the First World War in 1914 and the Bolshevik Revolution in 1917. Pending a settlement, although the Mir of Hunza made several attempts to reassert his claims on the Raskam valley, the Government of India took no steps in the direction of its reoccupation. At the end of the First World War, therefore, India emerged not with the Ardagh line as Lamb (p. 110) has supposed but with the Mustagh-Aghil-Qara Tagh-Kuen Lun Line up to which alone *de facto* occupation now extended and to the south of which the Chinese had been unable to encroach ever since the adoption of their forward policy in 1890. Lamb admits (p. 112) that the Chinese never exercised administration in Aksai Chin but thinks that from

[26]S.F. February 1913, p. 5/n.

the Indian side no one except the occasional explorer, big-game hunter, and nomad visited the region before 1950. He forgets to recognize, however, that in uninhabited areas such visits are sufficient to establish continuity of title and jurisdiction.

In 1927 there was some discussion regarding frontier areas, particularly in the north of Kashmir, which were under regular administration, but no final decision as such was taken regarding the external boundary. It was in 1936 that the Government of India finally advised the Mir of Hunza to stop the practice of exchanging presents with the Chinese Government and formally to relinquish his rights over the Taghdumbash and Raskam areas. The Government of independent India, which inherited the *de facto* boundary as it had emerged by 1947, got the whole question re-examined and found that, notwithstanding the existence of genuine claims up to the Kuen Lun, the previous governments had in practice relinquished these claims voluntarily and that the international boundary had crystallized along the Mustagh-Aghil-Qara Tagh-Kuen Lun Line. They decided to respect this line as it coincided also with the Mustagh and Aghil watersheds. The maps which were still showing the original effective border as it existed prior to 1890 up to the Kuen Lun were now revised to show the new *de facto* boundary. At the same time, steps were taken to establish more effective jurisdiction in such areas as Aksai Chin, which were uninhabited, by sending regular patrols.

The Government of Pakistan—which was in illegal occupation of the area west of the Karakoram pass since 1948—decided, in March 1963, either through ignorance of the history of the frontier question or, as is more likely, through political motives to cede the entire Shaksgam valley south of the Aghil range where the Mir of Hunza had never ceased to exercise jurisdiction. In doing so they ignored the fact that as late as 1938-39, there had been exchange of correspondence with the Chinese Government on this question and that the Government of India had reasserted its earlier position.

8

The North-East Frontier of India Before 1914

THE PROBLEM concerning the North-East Frontier of India can be better understood if things are seen in their proper perspective.

Here, the Great Himalayan Range varying in height from 15,000 to 22,000 feet separates the Tibetan plateau from the Indian subcontinent and, except in a few isolated places where the range is crossed by certain rivers, it forms a natural watershed and a geographical barrier. To the south of the range lies a belt of wooded hilly area inhabited in its narrow longitudinal valleys by backward tribal people, the direction of whose intercourse follows that of the rivers towards the plains of Assam. True, the Himalayas have not been a watertight barrier and Tibetan influence and religion have come down the valley in one or two places. But history is determined not by exceptions but by the general flow of events, and so also is a natural boundary determined by the general lay of the land. This is no mere vague generalization of principle, for it finds support in recorded history.

The history of this frontier is to be traced not from the British victory of Yandabo in 1826, but from much earlier times—the period of the Indian epics and the *Puranas* which contain significant references to the tribal people and their territories.[1] The ancient Indian kingdoms of Pragjyotisha and Kamarupa comprised much of the eastern cis-Himalayan territories including Bhutan and Tawang. The accounts of ancient travellers such as Hieun Tsang and even modern critical works like Cunningham's *The Ancient Geography*

[1]See *Report of the Indian Officials*, p. 103.

of India confirm this fact.[2] The Ahoms, who succeeded the early Hindu kings of Kamarupa, established extensive relations with the tribal people and there is evidence to show that they had a well-organized system to conduct relations with the tribal people. As in later British days the Ahoms had frontier officers whose job it was to control and conciliate the tribal people. A work of the seventeenth century entitled *Political Geography of the Assam Valley* refers to the Bhutiyas, the Akas, and the Daflas, and to the tributes paid by them to the Ahom kings. Similarly, Mughal historians and early British writers like Michell and Mackenzie recognize that Ahom sovereignty prevailed over the neighbouring hills.

This evidence regarding Ahom control over the tribal area receives indirect support from the complete absence of recorded evidence regarding Tibetan influence in these early days. Indeed, whatever little evidence is available about the external limits of Tibet in those days shows clearly that Tibet never controlled these areas. Thus Desideri, a Jesuit traveller who resided in Lhasa for several years between 1716 and 1729, refers to Tsari as lying on the extreme borders of Tibet, and states that further east of Tsari lay Congbo which marched with the "people called Lhoba, which means southern people.... Not even the Tibetans, who are close neighbours and have many dealings with them, are allowed to enter their country, but are obliged to stop on the frontier to barter goods."[3] Horace Della Penna, another traveller who visited Tibet a little later in 1730, wrote that Tibet "on the south is bounded by Bengal, Lho ten ke, Altibari, Mon, Brukpa, Lhoba, Lho K'haptra, Shabado, Bha...."[4]

But more significant than the above is the fact that none of the authoritative Chinese works of the eighteenth and nine-

[2]See *The Ancient Geography of India*, p. 500 and the map facing the title page.

[3]De Filippi, *An Account of Tibet: Travels of Desideri*, 1937, pp. 143-5.

[4]C.R. Markham, *Narratives of the Mission of George Bogle to Tibet and of the Journey of Thomas Manning to Lhasa*, London, 1879, p. 314. Mon mentioned above applied to Tawang and Lho K'haptra to the Lhoka area of Tibet.

teenth centuries such as the *Wei tsang tu chih* (1792) and *Hsi tsang tu kao* (1886) show any knowledge either of Tawang or of any of the tribal territories. On the other hand, they invariably refer to these areas as the land of the wild people—*Lao Kha*—which lay outside the domains of Tibet. Similarly, all Chinese maps, including those prepared in the time of Kang-hsi (1711-17) and the later Chings, show the entire tribal belt outside Tibet.

It is not surprising, therefore, that during the 1960 talks the Chinese could bring forward no historical evidence whatsoever in support of their claims except for some stray reports of incursions made into the Mishmi and Abor areas during the years following the campaign of Chao Erh-feng in 1910.

THE TAWANG TRACT

While on the basis of the above evidence one could safely reach the conclusion that the Chinese claims over the north-eastern frontier areas of India had no historical basis, there was one complicating factor which provided some foundation, however slender and unsubstantiated, of much argument in favour of so-called Tibetan influence and administration in one of the border areas, namely, Tawang. This was the effort made by the fifth Dalai Lama to renovate the Tawang monastery in about 1680. Before this period the Tawang monastery was in a state of decay or perhaps belonged to the Dukpa sect which was the sect prevalent also in neighbouring Bhutan. The renovation of the Tawang monastery in 1680 seems to have been followed by an increase in the power and influence of the Buddhist monks and, therefore, also of the Dalai Lama's religious jurisdiction. But territorially Tawang remained outside the temporal jurisdiction of the Dalai Lama and was ruled, by all accounts, by chiefs called Deb Rajas as in neighbouring Bhutan. There is no evidence to show that these chiefs were dependent on any Tibetan officials. On the other hand, these chiefs, like other tribal chiefs further south and east appear to have been in varying degrees of subordination and control of the Ahom kings.

The Assamese merchants used the Tawang route for purposes of Trade with Tibet. Hamilton writing in 1808 observed:

> At a place called Chouna, two months' journey from Lhasa, on the confines of the two States, there is a mart established, and on the Assam side there is a similar mart at Geegunshur, distant four miles from Chouna. An annual caravan repairs from Lhasa to Chouna, conducted by about 20 persons, conveying silver bullion to the amount of about one lakh of rupees, and a considerable quantity of rock salt for sale to the Assam merchants which is imported into Thibet from Assam in large quantities....[5]

In the later years of Ahom rule in the late eighteenth and early nineteenth centuries, as Ahom power declined, the Deb Rajas of Tawang became more independent and started leading marauding expeditions over the Darrang plains and levying exactions from the plains people. The Tawang chiefs were assisted in these expeditions by the other Bhutiya tribes inhabiting the areas south of the Se La, who while continuing to owe allegiance and to receive their allowances from the Assam Rajas were not averse to transfer allegiance, whenever it suited them, to the Tawang chief whose independence and power were growing day by day. There were three main groups of Bhutiyas, namely, the Sherchokpa living in the Dirang valley, the Sherdukpen of Shergaon and Rupa, and the Thebengias of Tembang, Konia, and But. Of these various groups the Sherchokpa together with the Tawang chief succeeded in course of time in establishing certain rights in the fertile Kuriapara *duar* adjoining Udalguri. The Sherdukpen and Thebengias similarly asserted rights in the *Charduar* areas east

[5]Cited in Mackenzie, *The North-East Frontier of Bengal*, 1884, p. 15.

of Kuriapara. The Bhutanese asserted rights over the seven *duars*—five in Kamrup and two in Darrang areas.[6]

Besides the Bhutanese and the Bhutiyas there were many others who advanced claims of various types. As Mackenzie observes:

> The British authorities who succeeded the Ahom rulers found the Assam valley surrounded on the north, east and south by numerous savage and warlike tribes whom the decaying authority of the Assam dynasty had failed of late years to control and whom the disturbed condition of the province had incited to encroachment. Many of them advanced claims to rights more or less definite over lands lying in the plains; others claimed tributary payments from the villages below their hills, or the services of paiks said to have been assigned them by the Assam authorities.[7]

The British tried to reconcile these claims as best as they could with the requirements of enlightened policy and to treat the tribes "fairly and liberally."[8] In a good number of cases they allowed the tribes to continue enjoying their rights and allowances, provided they observed the terms on which the original rights and allowances were based, namely, restraint from acts of plunder and devastation. But wherever the tribes defaulted the British did not hesitate to revoke the concessions and to enforce law and authority. Thus between 1826 and 1844, when they found that the *duars* were being mismanaged and subjected to oppression and depredation, they were forced to resume direct administration. In 1841

[6]These *duars*, which on the Assam side were nine in all, together constituted a narrow tract of fertile land, varying in breadth from ten to twenty miles, between the base of the hills and the Assam plains. The possession of the *duars* was coveted by the people of the hills because they were dependent to a considerable extent on the products, such as rice and cotton, of these *duars*.

[7]Mackenzie, *The North-East Frontier of Benga* , p. 7.

[8]*Ibid.*, p. 6.

the seven *duars* hitherto held by the Bhutanese, and in 1844 the Kuriapara *duar* held by the Tawang and Sherchokpa Bhutias, were resumed and compensation paid to each of them.

Lamb[9] has advanced the view that the payment of compensation indicated that the lands in question were held by the tribes in original right. This view has no basis in documents. On the other hand, there is evidence to show that whatever rights were exercised by the tribes, whether in the form of receipt of allowances or of holding of lands, they were always conditional on good behaviour or payment of tribute. Thus, the allowance of Rs. 2,526-7-0 paid to the Sherdukpen was withheld for misconduct in 1839. It was restored partially in 1844 and fully in 1852. The Bhutanese, who had held the seven western *duars*, were required to pay an annual tribute of Rs. 4,785. The Tawang Bhutiyas held Kuriapara as the price of their forbearance from constant acts of plunder and violence. At the time of sanctioning the compensation of Rs. 5,000 to the Tawang Bhutiyas, the Secretary to the Government of India in his letter dated 12 October 1842 told Major Jenkins, Agent to the Governor General:

> I am directed to remind you that in entertaining the question of compensation to the Bhooteea Rajahs the Government *does not in the least degree recognize an original right* on their part to the possession of the Dooars. It is doubtful if they ever had any such right—a liberty of ranging over those rich tracts for certain months in the year was probably all that they possessed, and this was conceded to them by the old rulers of Assam as the price of their forbearance from constant acts of plunder and violence. As a measure of policy, therefore, though not demanded by justice, the Government is willing to allow the Bhooteea Rajahs such pecuniary compensation as may in some measure reconcile them to their loss, and may be so far appreciated by them,

[9] *The China-India Border*, p. 118; see also *McMahon Line*, II, p. 304.

that they would not risk forfeiting it, by aggression on the Dooars.[10]

After the resumption of Kuriapara in 1844 British hold over the Bhutiya communities had been considerably strengthened. Both the Sherdukpen, whose allowances were restored in part in 1844, and the Thebengias, who were in receipt of an allowance of Rs. 145-13-6, remained friendly. The Sherdukpen pledged themselves in 1844 "to act up to any orders we may get from the British authorities" and to submit all civil disputes to the British courts. Similarly, the Tawang Bhutiyas remained friendly until 1853 when one of their officials, a Gelling, deputed to receive the annual pension of Rs. 5,000 failed to forward this amount to Tawang and took refuge in Darrang. The Deb Raja of Tawang sent armed guards to demand the surrender of the official, but eventually agreed not only to withdraw the demand but also to disband the guards he had mustered and to maintain peace on pain of forfeiting the pension of Rs. 5,000.

Some of the British officials like Mackenzie, who knew little about the early history of Tawang and the peculiar nature of administration that prevailed there, often failed to make a distinction between the temporal authority of the Deb Raja and the spiritual authority of the Tawang monastery and tended to mistake the one for the other. The cause of this confusion, no doubt, lay partly in the fact that the monastery which had by now acquired considerable private properties and had employed a hierarchy of officials for their management had set up an administration, of its own, parallel to that of the Deb Raja. In course of time, its power and influence had increased to such an extent and its spiritual hold over the Deb Raja had become so firm that people tended to consider the latter subordinate to the former. And as the monastery in turn took its orders from Lhasa, Tawang itself came to be looked upon as some sort of a dependency of Tibet. This

[10]Foreign Dept. Consultations 12 October 1842, No. 81.

was an impression which was not disadvantageous to the Deb Raja, for while, on the one hand, Lhasa did not make any attempt to transform its spiritual control into a temporal one, on the other hand, it enabled him to acquire a better bargaining position *vis-a-vis* the British. Thus it is that in 1853 he ventured to send his armed guards to Kuriapara and the guards came to be characterized as a "Tibetan force." There was in fact no such "Tibetan" force and even the Chinese during the 1960 talks did not claim that any such "Tibetan" army had been despatched. On the other hand, the Chinese only contended that "the Tawang monastery, and the Babu and headmen of the borders" wrote a letter of assurance stating that "we will never waver in our loyalty" to the Dalai Lama. This "letter of assurance" was written with reference to the undertaking that the Deb Raja had given to the British in 1853. The Deb Raja was not a signatory to this letter. Only the Abbot and monastic officials stationed at Talung Dzong and other places had signed it. It is inconceivable that the Chinese would have failed to make a reference to the political submission, if any, made by the Deb Raja to the Government of Tibet at this time or to the despatch of a Tibetan force earlier in 1853. This is a significant omission proving as it does the fact that the temporal authority of the Deb Raja was still independent of Tibetan control.

The demarcation of the Bhutiya tribal boundary with Assam in 1873 has been characterized by Lamb[11]—and he was right in thinking that this would cause some surprise—as some sort of international demarcation between India and Tibet. Lamb's sole basis in arriving at this startling conclusion is the fact that some officials whom he characterizes both as "monastic" and "Tibetan" happened to be present when a British official who was deputed to demarcate the Indo-Bhutan boundary utilized the occasion to lay down also the limits of the Bhutiya tribal territory with Assam. Lamb overlooks the fact that the Bhutiyas, who were imme-

[11]*The China-India Border*, p. 121; see also *McMahon Line*, II, p. 301.

diately concerned in this demarcation, were the Sherdukpen who had always remained under Indian jurisdiction both during the Ahom and the British days and were in continuous enjoyment, except during 1839-44, of an annual pension of Rs. 2,526-7-0. The priests, who were present on the occasion, were apparently from the Tawang monastery and even if they were Tibetan they had no formal authority. No correspondence had been exchanged between the Government of India and the Government of Tibet and no enquiries had been made regarding the credentials, the precise official status, or even the nationality of the priests. The demarcation of this boundary was, therefore, no more "international" in character than the demarcation of any other tribal or district boundary in India. Indeed, a notification issued on 8 March 1876 declared this very line "as defined in the Revenue Survey in the years 1872-73-74-75, and demarcated by pillars Nos. 98 to 160 inclusive" as the *Inner Line* in the Darrang area. Lamb does not dispute the fact that the *Inner Line* was always considered as an administrative line and not an external boundary.

Lamb admits that even as late as 1914 the Tsona Dzongpons exercised no jurisdiction whatsoever in the territory south of the Se La, and that this entire stretch with the exception of Senge Dzong, which was a private estate of the Tsona Dzongpons, was owned and administered by the Tawang monastery. But north of the Se La, he thinks, there was some sort of dual control by the Tsona Dzongpons and the Tawang monastery. How did this peculiar system come into existence? What happened to the Deb Raja to whose rule we find frequent references in earlier writings? Why were not the Tsona Dzongpons or the Tawang monastery mentioned as parties to the agreement of 1844 if either of them had any temporal hold over Tawang or its possessions at that period? Through what process was the authority of the Deb Raja and the Sat Rajas of the Dirang-chu valley come to be eliminated and later substituted by that of the Tawang monastery? In the answers to these questions lies the key to the understanding of the Tawang problem and

Lamb has made no attempt either to ask these questions or to view the evidence on Tawang critically.

It would appear that the final usurpation of the temporal authority of the Deb Raja by the priestly hierarchy of the Tawang monastery took place some time after 1853, for it is after that date that the Deb Raja ceases to find mention in documents. But the Tawang monastery continued to be independent of any temporal control from Tibet and it so far guarded its own position as to prevent the entry of Tibetans even on the pretext of trade. Nain Singh, travelling in the area during 1874-75, notes that Tibetan traders were not permitted entry beyond "the limit of the Tsona Dzongpons jurisdiction" which lay at Chukhang, a customs post, a few miles south of Tsona, and that the monastery not only had its own monastic council and administrative officials called Gelengs and Nerpas, but also its own guards to defend the territories.[12] It is likely, however, that at a later period the monastery hired the services of the Tsona Dzongpons for the management of its affairs, for at the time of the Simla Conference, Lonchen Shatra referred to the income which the *Potala Trung-yik* chempo and the Loseling College of the Drepung monastery received from Tawang in lieu of the services rendered by its agents (the Tsona Dzongpons) in the management of the Tawang lands, and made a specific request that such income received from Tawang might be considered as the income of private individuals.

THE TRIBES OF EAST ASSAM

While Tawang, despite its political independence, had been subjected to some cultural and religious influences from the north, the tribal people living further east were, with the exception probably of a handful of them in the extreme north of the Dihong valley, almost completely free from any Tibetan influence. The large majority of these tribal people lived

[12]*Records of the Survey of India,* Vol. III, pt. I, pp. 178-9.

in the lower hills adjoining the Assam plains, along the valleys of the rivers Bhareli, Ranga, Subansiri, Dihong, Dibong, and Zayul. The upper courses of these rivers lay in areas which were higher in altitude, difficult of access, and thickly wooded. They were separated from the Tibetan plateau by the Great Himalayan Range which had but a few passes. The Tibetan provinces adjoining them were backward and unproductive. On the other hand, the plains of Assam in the south were rich and fertile and there were innumerable rivers and streams in the foothills skirting the plains which afforded a safe and convenient haven for tribal settlements. The concentration of the tribal people, therefore, tended to be heavier in the southern valleys and the direction of their intercourse, both political and cultural, tended to follow these river valleys towards Assam.[13]

The Ahoms during the six hundred years of their rule seem to have been far more successful in their dealings with the tribes than the British were during the early years of their rule in the nineteenth century. Contemporary Assamese accounts describe the well-organized system that the Ahoms had set up to control the tribal population, and both Mughal and British accounts testified to the fact that many of these tribes had tendered submission and even taken up service in the Ahom army. The Mughal historian, Shihabuddin Talish, wrote: "Although most of the inhabitants of the neighbouring hills pay no tax to the Rajah of Assam, yet they accept his sovereignty and obey some of his commands."

Michell, a British officer, wrote in 1883: "Before we took possession of Assam, the Mishmis were obedient to the orders

[13]Lamb (p. 122) cites Sir Robert Reid to say that none of these tribes was "Indian" in origin, outlook, etc. It seems hardly necessary to refute this, for it is as unnecessary to prove their Indian nationality at this stage as to prove the British nationality of the Scottish highlanders. India is a huge country and there are a good number of aboriginals in different parts of the country, who are as much native to the Indian soil as the people of any other province. Surely, the tribes of the North-East Frontier are far more akin to the Indians than the Tibetans are to the Chinese.

of the Assam Government and paid tribute to the Sadiya Khowa Gohains."[14] Similarly, about the Abors, Michell noted: "1825—Captain Neufville reported to the Quarter-Master General that the Abors were giving assistance to the Gohain of Sadiya against the Singphos" (p. 53). He also stated that "a large body of them, to the amount of 20,000 or 30,000 came down to assist the Bura Gohain in repelling the Maomarias, who were devastating all the country east of Jorhat" (p. 55).

The above account would show that the policy of the Ahom rulers was not only to check depredations through a system of "bribes and subsidies" but also to extend political control and to obtain the willing co-operation of the tribal people in the defence and administration of the frontier areas. In maintaining control over the tribal people it was scarcely necessary for the Ahoms to penetrate deep into the hills, for a majority of the tribal people, and in particular the more important sections of them, lived along the foothills and not deeper down. The submission of these sections of tribes automatically ensured control over other sections living in the interior.

As observed earlier, it is only in the later years of their rule that the Ahoms lost control over the tribes and the latter advanced a number of claims. The British Government dealt with these claims in a liberal and conciliatory manner and agreed in many cases to continue the system of payment of allowances on condition of good behaviour. Wherever the tribes failed to behave, they imposed blockades and sent punitive expeditions to enforce order. The Akas and the Mishmis were easily reconciled to these policies. But the Daflas and Abors often created trouble and necessitated several expeditions. In none of these troubles created by the Abors and Daflas, however, had the Tibetans any hand and it would be absurd to suggest that such temporary recalcitrance of the tribal people rendered their territory in any way non-Indian. The entire tribal territory up to the limit of

[14]Michell, *Report on the North-East Frontier of India*, 1883, p. 97

Tibetan control continued as heretofore to be treated as Indian and if the British did not think in terms of physical occupation of the area, it was only because there was no threat or possibility of any external influence or control being extended over the area. The various undertakings given by the tribal people, the coercive action taken by the British Government to compel them to abide by their undertakings, and the laws and regulations passed from time to time show that the British always retained the power not only of influencing but also of controlling the tribal people.

INNER LINE AND OUTER LINE

During 1872-73, the Government of India extended to Assam the application of Statutes 32 and 33 Vic, Cap 3, whereby the government was enabled to assume powers of summary legislation for backward tribes. The first use to which the government put this power of summary legislation was to pass the "Bengal Eastern Frontier Regulation-I of 1873" empowering the provincial government to prescribe what was known as the *Inner Line* beyond which people were to be prohibited from visiting or acquiring any proprietary interests. The object of this regulation was not only to prevent friction between the plains people and the tribal people but also to prevent explcitation of the tribal areas, and the evasion of taxes which were still exempt in such territories.

Notifications describing the *Inner Line* in the Lakhimpur and Darrang districts were issued in September 1875 and March 1876 respectively. The *Inner Line* in the Darrang area followed the boundary demarcated in 1873 up to pillar 160. East of this pillar, it followed a specially defined alignment up to the Lakhimpur district boundary at Mora Sessa river. The major part of this alignment lay along the foothills. The *Inner Line* in the Lakhimpur area ran not along the foothills but along certain artificial though well-marked features. These consisted of embankments, patrol paths, and the courses of rivers (see Map 6).

Beyond the newly defined *Inner Line* of the Lakhimpur district, there lay a tract of land up to the foothills which had originally been inhabited by the Miris but which, through frequent depredations of the Abors, had now become practically uninhabited. The Miris had crossed over to the southern side of the *Inner Line*. In the undertakings given during the years 1863-66, the Abors had recognized that this tract lying to the south of the foothills formed a regular part of the British administered districts. After the definition of the *Inner Line* of 1875, this line along the foothills sometimes came to be called rather vaguely as the *Outer Line*. The precise points followed by this *Outer Line* were never defined, but the line had been delineated roughly on a map prepared by Needham, the first Assistant Political Officer, appointed to deal with the Abor tribes. Later on, this term, the *Outer Line*, gained currency and found its way into some of the maps. Since the Survey of India was in the practice of denoting the undemarcated district boundary by a symbol different than that used for the demarcated district boundary, the so-called *Outer Line* (which was different from the *Inner Line*) in the Lakhimpur area and the district boundary in the Darrang area (which, however, coincided with the *Inner Line*) came to be delineated by different symbols. The precise significance of the various symbols used was explained in a letter (dated 11 March 1904) from the Government of India to the Chief Commissioner of Assam. The letter stated:

> The symbol to be ordinarily adopted in the case of provincial frontiers should be dash-dot-dash (—.—.—) line, and this should be employed wherever the boundary has been settled by inter-provincial arrangement or by demarcation.
>
> Where a territorial boundary though undemarcated is settled by treaty, or is acknowledged in practice, it should be indicated as an approximate boundary by a plain broken line.
>
> Where the territorial boundary of the province has not been determined either by inter-provincial agreement, by

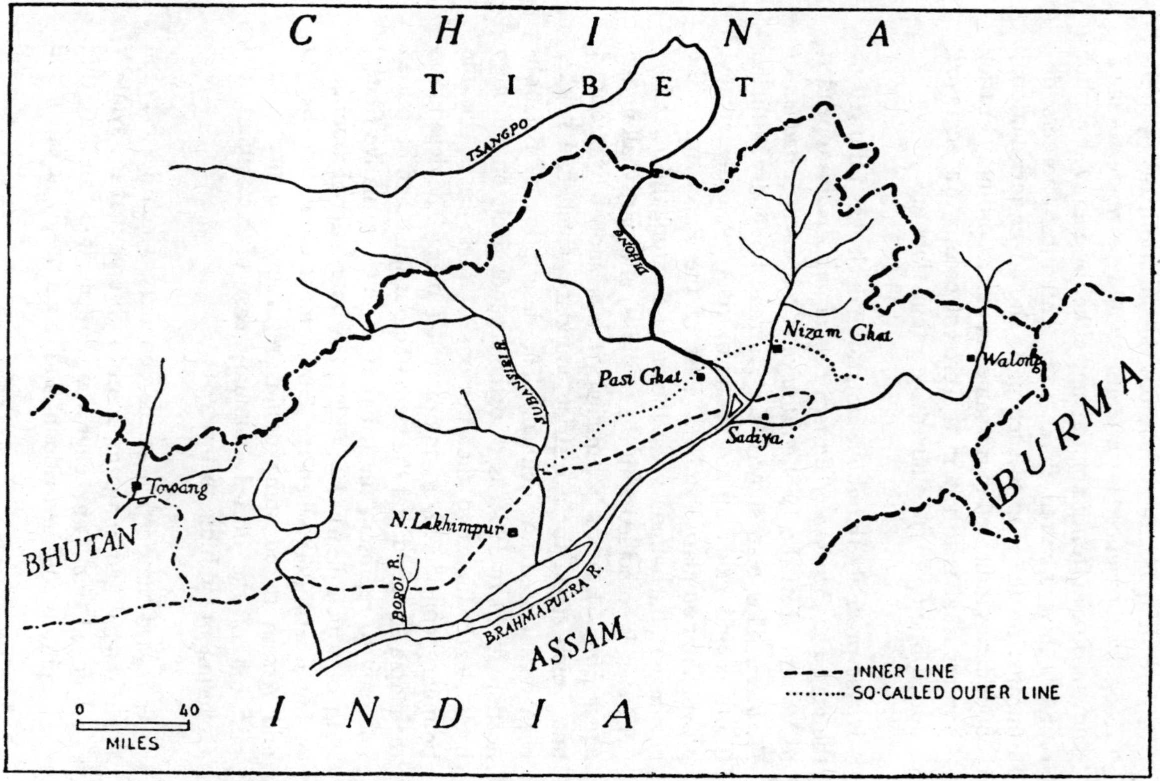

MAP 6. The North-East Frontier of India illustrating the *Inner Line* and the so-called *Outer Line*

demarcation, by treaty without demarcation, or by well-recognized practice, no attempt should be made to show any territorial frontier on the map either by engraved symbol or by any coloured band. The outermost borders delineated on the map in such parts should be jurisdictional boundaries indicated in the same manner as ordinary district borders, that is to say in the present case by an engraved dotted line (.....) coloured by a thin ribbon.[15]

It was precisely the above notation which was followed in the map *The Province of Eastern Bengal and Assam* appended to Volume II of the 1909 edition of Aitchison's *Collection of Treaties.* This map showed the Darrang boundary with the Bhutiyas and Akas up to the Baroi river by a demarcated provincial boundary symbol. East of the Baroi up to the Nizamghat, the boundary was shown partly along the *Inner Line* (wherever it coincided with the foothills) and partly along the *Outer Line.* East of Nizamghat, it was shown by a dotted line which stood for a district boundary which had neither been demarcated nor defined. The description of the notification given in 1904 as also the legend given on the map itself clearly indicated that in none of these cases was the boundary considered an international one. The legend on the map also stated that the yellow colour-wash had been used not only to represent the tribal areas but also native States, both of which clearly lay within the international boundary of India. In 1908 when the Government of Eastern Bengal and Assam raised some doubts regarding the precise implication of the dotted boundary east of Nizamghat, the Government of India reaffirmed:

As regard the portion of the boundary which lies between Nizamghat and Sangsam, I am to observe that the symbols employed, viz. "an engraved dotted line and a thin continuous coloured ribbon" indicate a purely jurisdictional

[15]E.A. April 1904, No. 31.

or administrative line and not a definite territorial boundary. This portion of the boundary is, therefore, correctly indicated, as directed in paragraph 3 of the letter from the Government of India in the Foreign Department, No. 820-EB dated 11 March 1904, and it is not apparent how the colour line can be regarded as constituting an authoritative description of the boundary of British India or of the Province of Assam.[16]

Contrary to the assertion made by Lamb,[17] therefore, "even the most casual research" shows that the foothills were never recognized as an international border. The British Government had resorted to this practice of representing the tribal territory by a colour-wash because while they undoubtedly considered the tribal belt as lying within the external boundary of India, they had not yet been able to conduct surveys and to ascertain the precise alignment of such an external boundary. It is for this reason that when in 1880 the Assam Frontier Tracts Regulations giving the Chief Commissioner of Assam certain special powers over the tribal areas was passed, the Government found it inadvisable to define the outer boundaries of the tribal tract. The Chief Commissioner of Assam in his letter of 12 July 1879 stated:

> I am to observe that, in specifying the tracts to which the Regulation should apply, no clear definition of boundaries, at least of the boundary most distant from the settled part of the adjoining district, is possible. It would only be practicable, or indeed necessary, to define clearly the boundary which is to separate the non-regulation tract from the district it adjoins.

[16]E.A. June 1908, No. 26.

[17]*The China-India Border*, pp. 126-7; *McMahon Line*, II, pp. 313-5. (Incidentally, the confusion in Lamb's mind regarding the *Outer Line* concept has resulted in his depicting two different versions of it in Maps 11 and 16 of his book, *The China-India Border*.)

Accordingly, the notifications issued under the above Regulation in 1884 and 1914, while describing in detail the boundary of the frontier tracts with the administered districts, gave no description of the external boundaries of those tracts.

RELATIONS WITH TIBET

As against these specific administrative arrangements undertaken by the British we seldom come across any instances of Tibetan control or organized attempts at administration in any of these areas in the nineteenth century. Indeed, except for the Tawang area where, as already seen, Tibetan spiritual influence prevailed, even the Chinese were unable during the 1960 talks to cite instances of Tibetan control. The Tibetans certainly paid no subsidies, obtained no undertakings, and had devised no system of political control. In fact, the nature of Tibetan administration that prevailed in the adjoining areas of Poyul and Zayul was itself so rudimentary in character and central control over them so loose and intermittent that the question of Tibetan control over the *Loba* territory never arose.

It has been seen earlier that the main concentration of tribal settlements were in the areas adjoining the plains of Assam and that there was a steady movement from the upper valleys towards the south. Thus, the Miris who once inhabited the middle Dihong valley had migrated to the foothills and the plains, and their places had been taken by the Abors. The places vacated by the Abors in turn were filled by the Monbas who came from Bhutan and Tawang "in search of a land of promise which ancient prophesies had called Pemako and which was believed to be near the frontiers of India." The land occupied by the Monbas became in later years subject to occasional depredations and exactions both from the unruly Pobas in the north and the Abors in the south, but it would hardly be proper to consider such tribal raids as evidence of control from either side. The Monbas continued to be as distinct and independent of either as indeed the Pobas continued to be independent of Tibetan control. Apart from the Dihong valley a section of the Monbas occupied also the upper Siyom valley which was known as the *Pachakshiri* region. Here the rich Lhalu family of Tibet happened to own some private estates and the *pachakshiribas* had to pay rent in lieu of the land held from this family. The two other areas where the Tibetans came into contact with the tribes were the Mipi area in the Dibong valley and the Walong area in the Zayul valley. In both these areas, which were very small in extant, the Tibetans came as refugees whom the local Mishmis employed as slaves or servants to look after their herds.

In the Subansiri area where the routes of the two pilgrimages—the *Kingkor* and the *Ringkor*—were located, contact between the Tibetans and the *Lobas* (the local Tagins) were rare. A belt of about 15 to 20 miles area between Migyitun and the Subansiri valley was almost entirely uninhabited and it was only once in twelve years when the Tibetan pilgrims came along the Tsari-chu for the *Ringkor* pilgrimage that they encountered the Tagins in the Subansiri valley. On such occasions they propitiated the Tagins with presents of Tsampa, salt, and swords. These were *ad hoc* arrangements made at long intervals and bore no comparison with the system of annual subsidies through which the British exercised control over the tribal people.

Except for the above isolated areas, which marched with Tibet along some 60 to 75 miles at the most and where some sort of contact had necessarily to exist between two neighbours, over the rest of the nearly 600 miles of Indo-Tibetan border in this region there was, and indeed could be, no contact, much less influence or control, from the Tibetan side over the tribal people in the cis-Himalayan regions. Even along the 60 or 75 miles of border noted above, contact was possible only during a few months of the year when the high passes, varying from altitudes 14,000 to 18,000 feet, were free from snow. The tribal people were, therefore, compelled to follow the natural inclination of the land and the direction of the valleys they inhabited towards the plains of Assam where alone their requirements could be met in full. This makes nonsense of the so-called horizontal stratification of tribes. The stratification was always longitudinal and people belonging to particular tribal groups were to be found along individual valleys lying north-south and not along a multitude of valleys. Such manipulation of trade as existed worked to the detriment of the Tibetans rather than of the tribes, for while access from Tibet was confined to a few particular passes, access to Assam was possible through a multitude of paths. Thus, the Bhutiyas, both of Tawang and the regions further south, the various sections of the Abors (Boris, Minyong, and Padam), all along the Dihong valley, and the Mishmis of the Dibong and Zayul valleys seldom had trouble in getting access to the markets of Assam. We have seen earlier that the Tawang people had been successful in preventing access of Tibetan merchants south of the Chukhang customs post, lying five miles south of Tsona. Similarly, there is evidence to show that the Abors were in the habit of blocking Tibetan ingress along the Dihong. Michell wrote:

> Father Desgodin, who resided many years in Thibet, believes that these people of Poba would be only too glad to trade with neighbouring countries; but they are completely isolated by the mountain barriers surrounding them, which are inhabited by wild tribes.[18]

Major Ottley writing as late as 1906 observed:

> The situation at the present time is indeed a sad one and is thus. The large Tibetan population, above Gya La Jong in the Sang Po valley, are land and mountain bound. They have to get their tea and other necessaries of life either from China, at least 400 miles to the east, or over the Jelap, 500 miles to the west. They long for the Sang Po route to Sadiya to be opened up, which would bring

[18]Michell, *op. cit.*, p. 89.

them within 150 miles of all their necessaries of life, and the waterway to Calcutta. They cannot do it themselves, as they lack military combination and enterprise to crush the tribes blocking the road, viz. the Bor or Hill Abors, who for their own benefit will not allow Tibetans to come south through their country without paying enormous blackmail, in order that they may retain to themselves the monopoly of selling goods to the Tibetans at high prices. As the country on the west of the Dehong in Bhutan is inaccessible, the Tibetans cannot get out that way either, unless they go a long way round, and then they would have to pay the Bhutanese toll also. There is, therefore, friction between the Tibetans and the Bor Abors.[19]

BRITISH POLICY AND TRIBAL AUTONOMY

While thus the tribal people were free from Tibetan control, the absence of any deep penetration of the tribal areas by British officials in the nineteenth century is sometimes advanced as evidence of the existence of a sort of no man's land in the area. This is based on a misunderstanding of the manner in which British policy towards Indian States and tribal areas in general evolved. The British did not necessarily annex every State or region they conquered or subdued. A large number of Indian States, numbering more than six hundred, continued to enjoy various degrees of autonomy and to lead a separate existence right up to 1947. The tribal areas in the north-west as well as the north-east corresponded in some degree to these native States. British paramountcy over them was never questioned and the degree of control that the government was prepared to exercise depended on the exigencies of policy. In the north-west frontier, the Durand Line was demarcated as late as 1893, but the tribal belt up to this line was being controlled in various ways right from the middle of the nineteenth century. Similarly, in the north-east frontier,

[19]S.E. August 1907, 358-359-Appendix I to notes.

although the precise alignment of the frontier was laid down only in 1914, the tribes south of this line which were concentrated near the foothills were, as seen already, under various degrees of political control for several decades earlier. This control, it is true, was not such as would involve the physical occupation of the tribal territory. The government was opposed as a matter of policy to any intensification of control involving additional responsibilities on the administration. Nevertheless, there were any number of occasions when the government was compelled much against its own will to undertake such responsibilities. These were brought about mostly by the actions of the local authorities. Up to 1882, for example, the Deputy Commissioners were in the habit of dealing with the tribes through the medium of native officers who had great influence over the tribes. But after that year the appointment of a police officer, by name Needham, as Assistant Political Officer and his unfortunate marriage with a Miri woman led to a series of incidents with the Abors. In 1893 and in 1900 punitive expeditions had to be sent against the Abors and the Mishmis respectively and their territories blockaded for several years. After 1900 there was pressure from timber companies and tea plantations for intensification of control over the tribes and for advancing the *Inner Line* towards the north. The provincial authorities were inclined to support these measures. But the Government of India and the Secretary of State firmly opposed it and advised the provincial authorities not to undertake any action which would lead to conflict with the tribes. They had no objection, however, to the Assistant Political Officer touring the areas beyond the *Outer Line*, "provided it can safely be made without risk of conflict with the tribes." The provincial authorities were inclined to interpret this latter advice rather liberally and were responsible ultimately for creating a situation which led to the murder of Williamson and Gregorson in the Abor territory in March 1911. Ever since the 1893 expedition the Abors were ill prepared to suffer any encroachment on their autonomy and they took their revenge on these two unfortunate officers.

CHINESE THREAT: REVISION OF POLICY

This incident was undoubtedly responsible for a rethinking in government's policy towards the tribal area, but far more than this it was the external threat that was now developing that ultimately shaped the precise course of policy.

We have seen earlier that Britain, obsessed by Russophobia, had induced China to occupy a large tract of land, hitherto disclaimed by her, in southern Sinkiang. By the same obsession Britain had been impelled in 1906 to reimpose on Tibet the suzerainty of China which had by this time been practically non-existent for a long time. China, encouraged by this support, had proceeded through forceful diplomacy as well as military activity to convert her suzerainty into sovereignty. Her General Chao Erh-feng had reduced the whole of eastern Tibet between 1905 and 1910 and had now pushed through to Lhasa and forced the Dalai Lama to flee to India. Shortly afterwards the Chinese troops indulged in a series of aggressions along the Indian frontier. Rima was occupied and orders issued to the Mishmis to offer allegiance and to cut a road down to Assam. A body of troops entered the Pomed district of Tibet and threatened to march into Abor territory. Another party sneaked into the Aka country.

The Government of India considered the situation both in the above context and that of Williamson's murder in the Abor area and recommended to the Secretary of State, in July 1911, the despatch of a punitive expedition to the Abor area and a friendly mission to the Mishmi territory. It was proposed that the expedition to the Abor area should be utilized also for "such surveys and exploration as may be possible in order that we may obtain the knowledge requisite for the determination of a suitable boundary between India and China in this locality." Later, on 21 September 1911, the Government of India proposed:

> that endeavour should be made to secure, as soon as possible, a sound strategical boundary between China-cum-

Tibet and the tribal territory from Bhutan up to and including the Mishmi country, and this should, we consider, now be the main object of our policy. As long as such tribal territory lay between us and our peacefully dormant neighbour Tibet, an undefined mutual frontier presented neither inconvenience nor danger. With the recent change in conditions, the question of a boundary well defined and at a safer distance from our administrative border has become one of imperative importance and admits of no delay.

These proposals were duly sanctioned and were followed by a series of expeditions which conducted a thorough survey of the Mishmi, Abor, and Aka areas, and collected valuable information regarding the limits of Tibetan jurisdiction.

THE SIMLA CONFERENCE

By the time the various missions completed the investigations in the tribal area, the situation in Tibet had undergone a complete change. The power that Chao Erh-feng had tried to build through years of military campaigns received a sudden set-back. Tibet, taking advantage of the Chinese revolution of 1911, rose in revolt, expelled the Chinese troops, and issued a declaration of independence. Attempts made by the new Republican Government of China to reassert its authority evoked sharp reaction both from the Tibetan and the British Governments. In a Memorandum dated 17 August 1912 the British Government made it clear that it would not tolerate any further attempts by the Chinese Government to change the political status of Tibet from what had been stipulated in the treaties of 1904 and 1906. The Chinese Government at first refused to accept this position but later, as it became increasingly clear that conditions both in China and Tibet had made a reimposition of Chinese authority in Tibet practically impossible, found in the terms offered by Britain a convenient means of keeping up, in theory, at least a semblance of authority which it had found itself unable to assert in practice.

She, therefore, accepted the 17 August 1912 Memorandum as a basis for negotiations and entered the Simla Conference in the autumn of 1913. The negotiations at the conference were for a time bogged down in a controversy regarding the precise alignments to be adopted for Inner and Outer Tibet, but the terms finally initialed on 27 April 1914 practically confirmed the position stated in the 17 August Memorandum so far as Tibet's political status was concerned.

In so far as the Convention sought to place a limit on the extent to which China could interfere in the internal administration of Tibet, it was certainly of some importance to the Indo-Tibetan border. But of far greater importance than the Convention, for this purpose, was the Indo-Tibetan Agreement of March 1914 which laid down in clear terms the Indo-Tibetan boundary in a map on scale 1":8 miles. The Chinese later contended that this agreement was concluded behind the back of the Chinese representative and that they were not bound by it. This latter part of the contention seemed to be an unnecessary argument on their part, for in the circumstances in which the Simla Conference was held, Chinese approval or adhesion to an agreement entered into between India and Tibet was entirely redundant. At no time before 1951 had Tibet relinquished her right to have independent dealings with other powers or of entering into treaty relations with them. The draft Convention of 1914 had recognized this by empowering Tibet to conclude a separate treaty with Britain in regard to Indo-Tibetan trade regulations. As for the contention that the agreement was concluded behind the back of the Chinese representative, it seems extremely unlikely, as Lamb also recognizes, that the Chinese could have been unaware of the agreement. The proceedings of the conference do not indicate that the negotiations between the Indian and Tibetan representatives on this subject were held in secrecy and the fact that the Chinese made no protest when the agreement was published in Aitchison's volumes in 1929 shows that they were not only aware of its existence but that they had no objection to it.

9

Administering the North-East Frontier, 1914-1947

IT HAS BEEN seen earlier that while the *Inner Line* indicating some sort of an administrative line (beyond which the acquisition of properties was prohibited) was prescribed from time to time, the external boundary up to which British sovereignty extended was shown only by a rough colour-wash on maps and had not been precisely defined by the British. The so-called *Outer Line*, to which references were often found, did not indicate an external boundary. It referred only to the alignment of the foothills in the Lakhimpur area and was intended to distinguish this line from the *Inner Line* which lay further south in this particular sector. The Indo-Tibetan agreement of March 1914 defined for the first time the precise alignment of the external boundary of India in this region. This was done on the basis of information obtained during the two preceding years regarding the limits of Tibetan jurisdiction. Starting from the Bhutan boundary it followed the highest range[1] of the Himalayan mountains up to a point lying

[1]In 1962 the Chinese raised a controversy regarding the precise location of the McMahon Line in the Tawang Sector. They contended that the boundary delineated on the treaty map of March 1914 lay not along Thag La, the highest range in the area, but along Lat. 27° 44" 6' N which was south of Thag La. In doing so they ignored the fact that in actual practice it was Thag La and not Lat. 27° 44" 6' N which had been recognized as the traditional boundary by the local people. Indeed there were similar apparent discrepancies in certain other sectors of the McMahon Line. No fuss was made about them because they happened to be to China's advantage. People unfamiliar with survey and cartographic processes were easily taken in by Chinese propaganda. Between 1914 and 1962 a great deal of progress had been made in survey methods and while the actual location of the boundary on the ground as known and determined in 1914 continued to be the same its location in terms of co-

south of Subansiri. In the Subansiri and the Tsari areas, it departed from the highest watershed, but after Tsari it again ascended the watershed line. It crossed the Dihong river south of village Mongku and thereafter followed the northern watershed of the Dibong river. The line crossed the Zayul river a little south of Sama and joined the Burmese boundary near the Diphu pass.

TAWANG AND WALONG

The alignment thus defined included in Indian territory areas which had definitely been found to be lying outside Tibetan jurisdiction. In the earlier years, it is true, that doubts had been expressed regarding the precise political status of two of the areas, namely, Tawang and Walong, included in this territory. But fresh information showed that the doubts entertained earlier were not justified and that they were based only on misunderstanding of the peculiar nature of Tibetan influence that prevailed there. For example, about Tawang a report dated 11 November 1913 by Captain Nevill, Political Officer in charge of Western Section, North-East Frontier Tract, stated:

> The Towang district is cut off from Tibet proper by snow from December to June. The people are a very independent lot. They are called Monhpas. They differ very materially in language, dress, manner and appearance from the people of Tibet. In many respects they closely resemble the Drukpas (the inhabitants of Bhutan proper). The people are not ruled by the Jongpen of Chonajong, but are under the Towang kato, a sort of parliament composed of Lamas.... The Towang people are very jealous of their trade with Assam and have succeeded in keeping it entirely in their hands. Lhasa traders are not

ordinates on maps seemed to have varied in certain places. This was a mere theoretical difference which the Chinese thought fit to take advantage of for propaganda purposes.

permitted beyond the Chonajong jurisdiction, and all strangers are systematically prevented from passing through their country.[2]

Similarly, about Walong, a report dated 15 January 1912 from Dundas, Political Officer in charge of the Mishmi Mission, stated with reference to the earlier assertions regarding the existence of Tibetan authority in the Walong areas as follows:

> I cannot find any local corroboration or authority for this assertion. In my opinion Tibetan authority was never established so far south. It seems that Tibetans of the Zayul district were always nervous about their wild Miju neighbours.... Local evidence goes to show that Walong, Tine and Dong existed only on sufferance, because the people were useful to the Mijus in pasturing and looking after their cattle.[3]

Subsequently, W.M. Kennedy, Chief Secretary to the Chief Commissioner of Assam, reported on 17 September 1913:

> There was no question about this strip of land until the Chinese came and arbitrarily fixed their boundary at Menilkrai.
>
> Sati is the last Miju village on the right bank of the Lohit, and Sama the first old established Tibetan village. Almost midway between the two is one Tibetan house at Walong, which in the past was allowed to remain through the forbearance of the Mijus to whom this family of Tibetans was useful as a halting place on the journey to Rima, and also because they kept and pastured the Mijus cattle.
>
> The names of places, hills, flats and streams are Miju, and these are the names used by Tibetans who have none of their own for the Yepuk, Namti, Kraoti, Dunai, etc. The first Tibetan name met on the right bank of the Lohit, pro-

[2]S.E. September 1915, Enclosure to No. 87.
[3]S.E. May 1912, Enclosure to No. 278.

> ceeding north, is Tor Chu. Sama has neither cultivation nor any claims to land south of that stream.
>
> As a matter of fact the whole area is uninhabited (except for one house of Walong) from Sati stream to the Tor Chu and is a kind of Tom Tiddler's ground, belonging actually to the Mijus, who, however, for many years have no use for it.
>
> I went into this question carefully when I was in charge of the Mishmi Mission. Just the one visit of the Chinese to Menilkrai and the planting there of their flags, which indicate no boundary line, and the notification, has given rise to the belief that the land above as far as the Tor Chu cannot be claimed by us....
>
> The Chief Commissioner is of opinion that Mr. Dundas has furnished strong grounds for the conclusion that the Tor Chu falls within the sphere of the Mijus rather than that of the Tibetans.[4]

This report was confirmed shortly afterward on 8 February 1914 by another report sent by T.P.M. O'Callaghan who stated:

> It appears that after Dundas had returned in 1912, two Chinese officials with many followers came down and halted at Walong, and had the post put up. I am enquiring into the matter and have been joined by Walong, Tinai and Dong villagers. One thing is certain and that is that both the local Tibetans and the Mishmis admit that all rivers mapped as "Ti" (M'ju River, Water) have always been M'ju, and accordingly British territory.[5]

As the Chinese had no business to set up posts in what was decidedly Mishmi territory, Callaghan decided "to remove the posts to beyond the Tho Chu, as up to the right bank is admittedly our territory. This is admitted by the villagers

[4]S.E. September 1915, No. 76.

[5]S.E. September 1915, Enclosure to No. 96.

on both sides up to at least the Tho Chu on the right bank of the Lohit and to Kriti on the left bank."

On the basis of the above references, both the Assam Government and the Army Department advocatad that the boundary in this sector should lie just south of Sama. The Army Department adduced additional arguments in favour of this boundary on strategic grounds. They pointed out that the route from the Lohit valley to the Taluk pass on the Burma boundary lay along the Dichu stream.

PEMAKO AND TSARI

As for the Dihong Sector enquiries made during the recent surveys had shown that the whole of the Pemako region was once inhabited by Abors who had been driven south by the Pemakoibas. The latter had established their authority by now as far south as Kepang La. However, since the entire Poyul region of which Pemako formed a part had practically been independent of Tibetan control, both the Army Department and the Assam Government were inclined to claim a boundary north of Pemako. McMahon was reluctant to accept this advance line as it was bound to be disputed by the Tibetans. He, had, however, no hesitation in accepting a boundary south of village Mongku as he felt "we are on stronger ground and should have no difficulty in establishing Abor rights. Incidentally this line cuts the Dihang river as nearly as possible at the point where it ceases to be the Tsangpo and becomes the Dihang, a fact which itself speaks strongly for its ethnological correctness."

In the Subansiri area, the alignment of the boundary was based on an interim report which was submitted by Captain Bailey. He reported on the basis of local enquiries that Migyitun in the Tsari valley was the last Tibetan village and that Dru and Dro-tang in the Chayul valley were considered to be the frontier villages. Between Migyitun and the Chayul valley lay the route of the *Kingkor* pilgrimage along Chik Char, Droma La, Shagam La, and Potrang, which were regularly used by the Tibetans and were, therefore, considered as lying within Tibetan territory. The route of the longer pilgrimage called *Ringkor* lay entirely in Lopa territory and was used by the Tibetans once every twelve years only.

South of the Chayul valley, Bailey reported that the frontier lay along the crest of the Himalayan Range from Chupung La to Gori Chen peak.

C.A. Bell on behalf of the Government of India had detailed discussions with Lonchen Shatra about the proposed boundary between India and Tibet. Lonchen raised no objections and was apparently satisfied that the boundary shown on the map represented the actual territorial position between India and Tibet. He expressed some doubts, however, regarding the location of certain places of pilgrimage, namely, Tso-Karpo, Tsari Sarpa, and Tsari Nyingpa. The first two of these lay among the high mountains lying to the east of Migyitun. The third consisted of the two routes of pilgrimage *Kingkor* and *Ringkor* described earlier. The Lonchen was anxious that Tsokarpo and Tsari Sarpa as well as the *Kingkor* route should be left within Tibetan territory. As for the *Ringkor* route, he was only anxious that the village of Migyitun, where the pilgrims assembled once in twelve years before starting the pilgrimage, should be left in Tibetan territory. Bell assured him that this would be done. Apart from this, the only other points raised by Lonchen were regarding the ownership of private estates of po-Kanam Deba and the Lhalu family in the Dihong and Pachakshiri regions, and regarding the income that certain families were deriving from the Tawang monastery and other estates in that region. On these also, he was assured of non-interference.

TIBETAN ATTITUDE

After receiving these assurances, Lonchen referred the map to the Government at Lhasa and received their concurrence. The agreement was finalized through an exchange of notes on 24 and 25 March 1914. The points which had been raised by the

Tibetan Plenipotentiary as well as the assurances given by the British representative were duly recorded.[6]

Apart from the conditions mentioned in the agreement itself, the Tibetans apparently had no other reservations.[7] There is certainly no basis for the assumption that Tibet's agreement to the Indo-Tibetan boundary was conditional on the British securing a satisfactory Sino-Tibetan boundary, nor for the assumption that the Tibetans thought that they could continue with the "traditional conduct" of their administration south of the boundary agreed to. Neither the terms

[6]The interpretation given by Lamb (footnote on pp. 155-6 of his book) regarding the terms of the agreement are far from correct. The sacred places of Tsokarpo and Tsari Sarpa, which McMahon had promised to leave in Tibetan territory, were found by later surveys to lie outside the boundary agreed upon in 1914. They lay not to the south of Migyitun as Lamb assumes but to the east of it. The question of re-adjusting the boundary, therefore, did not arise. The references to the collection of dues by the Tibetan Government at Tsona and in Kongbu and Kham have been misinterpreted by Lamb to mean the collection of dues in Tawang and in the Dihong and Walong areas. There is no basis for this interpretation either in the exchange of notes or in the proceedings. McMahon's Note clearly stated that dues could be collected on goods sold by the Monpas and Lopas in Tibetan territory proper. Bell's Note dated 21 March 1914 regarding discussions with Lonchen stated: "The Lonchen then said that the Mon People at present pay taxes or duties on rice, chillies and other things which they bring for sale to Tsona Jong. Similar taxes or duties are also paid by the Lopas when they come to Kongbu and Kham and he asked whether the present arrangements may be continued. I said that all these are matters of detail which can be settled later on, on the receipt of the fuller information of revenue and expenditure which the Lonchen has promised to furnish."

[7]The note of the Tibetan Plenipotentiary dated 25 March 1914 in reply to McMahon's Note of 24 March stated: "As it was feared that there might be friction in future, unless the boundary between India and Tibet is clearly defined, I submitted the map, which you sent to me in February last, to the Tibetan Government at Lhasa for orders. I have now received orders from Lhasa, and I accordingly agree to the boundary as marked in red in the two copies of the maps signed by you, subject to the conditions mentioned in your letter, dated the 24th March, sent to me through Mr. Bell. I have signed and sealed the two copies of the maps. I have kept one copy here and return herewith the other."

of the agreement nor the proceedings of the conference justify such assumptions.

BRITISH TRIBAL POLICY UNAFFECTED

It is true that the conclusion of the agreement was not immediately followed by any substantial change in the nature of British administration in the frontier areas. This was due largely to the fact that the threat which the Chinese activities had posed during 1911-12 had now passed and the British Government saw no immediate need for incurring additional responsibilities in an area which was neither strategically nor financially of much consequence. Such Tibetan influence as existed in certain pockets of the frontier areas, it had been found during the surveys and tours of the years 1911-14, was not of a nature which necessarily contradicted British sovereignty and political control over these areas. In the Walong area, as has already been noted, except for the stray incidents of the Chinese attempts to mark an arbitrary boundary, there had never been any Tibetan administration. In the Pemako area the Tibetans had hardly been able to control even the Pobas over whom they claimed jurisdiction, and the prospect of their securing a foothold further south was remote. The Tawang area, no doubt, presented some complications. The reports of Bailey and Nevill had shown that, although Tawang had remained an independent unit and was clearly distinct administratively and ethnologically from Tsona, the employment of the services of the Tsona Dzongpons by the Tawang monastery in the management of its affairs was capable of being misinterpreted. The Lonchen had clarified the precise basis on which the services of the Tsona Dzongpons were being employed,[8] but it seemed

[8]The Lonchen had stated that the *Potala Trung-yik Chenpo* and the Loseling College of the Drepung monastery were each getting 10 Dotse (1 Dotse was equal to about Rs. 84) for their right to send Agents to manage the land of the Tawang monastery which right they farmed out to their Agents, and requested that such income might be considered as the income of private individuals.

necessary to prevent complications by making the presence of British administration also felt in Tawang. Both Bell and McMahon, therefore, recommended the appointment of a Political Officer for Tawang proper. But by this time the world war had broken out and Hardinge, the Viceroy, decided that the proposal should be in abeyance for the duration of the war. He agreed that "in the event of China making any serious endeavour to take advantage of our preoccupation, and give us trouble in regard to Tibet, we must make our dispositions when development occurs."

Without actually posting officers in the frontier areas, however, the Government of India took other measures designed to bring about a better definition of the nature of their administration in these areas, and to keep a closer watch both on inter-tribal relations and on external influences.

Prior to the agreement of 1914 the entire tribal area had been divided into three units, namely, the Central and Eastern Section, the Western Section, and the Lakhimpur Frontier Tract, each under a separate Political Officer. In 1914 the boundaries of these tracts with the districts of Assam were redefined and notifications issued to that effect.[9] The laws and regulations which were applicable to the tribal areas were also defined. The Government of Assam proposed the application of the Indian Penal Code, the Indian Arms Act, the first two sections of the Assam Land and Revenue Regulation, the Assam Forest Regulation, the Eastern Bengal and Assam Military Police Act, the Indian Police Act, the Scheduled Districts Act, the Whipping Act, and the Elephant Preservation Act. Proposals were also made for the extension of Section 144 of the Code of Criminal Procedure, and of Sections 22, 23, 38(2), and 40 of the Chin Hills Regulation, in a restricted and modified form. The Government of India approved

[9]In the Darrang area the newly defined alignment of the tract lay a little south of the *Inner Line* previously defined, and this led Lamb to conclude, though erroneously, that the latter was the *Outer* and the former the *Inner Line*. Actually no *Outer Line* was defined in this sector until March 1914.

all these with the exception of the Arms Act.[10] But it was explained "that in the administration of these territories the Political Officer and his Assistants will follow the spirit rather than the letter of the law. The rules which will be framed for their guidance will sedulously avoid anything in the shape of legal technicalities and will leave as far as possible to the local village authorities the punishment of all except heinous offences and the settlement of all civil disputes between natives of the tract."

These measures seemed to have proved popular with the tribes, for the administrative reports submitted by the Political Officers in subsequent years showed that the tribal people were turning more and more to the Political Officers for the settlement of their problems.

CHINESE MAPS, TIBETAN ACTIVITY, AND BRITISH CONSOLIDATION

It was not until the late 1930s that the Government of India were called upon to modify their policies. The Chinese who had hitherto remained indifferent and naturally unconcerned with the assertion of British sovereignty over the tribal areas started for the first time to put out feelers in the form of maps. These maps included a large part of eastern Tibet and the Indian tribal areas in the new Chinese province of Hsikang. The maps were unofficial and the boundaries shown in them bore no relation to the actual state of affairs. However, since these publications coincided with reports of illegal encroachments from Tibetan side, the Government of India found it necessary to revise their policy and to take more effective steps to make their authority felt. Fortunately, Tibetan activity was confined to two relatively small areas, namely, the upper Dihong valley and the Tawang area. In the Dihong valley, Tibetan activity was evidently of recent origin and of a casual nature and the British were able to

[10]E.A. April 1915, No. 7.

deal with this without much difficulty through more frequent tours of the Political Officers and through the establishment of outposts at Karko and Riga deep in the Abor territory in 1940 and 1941. The activities in the Tawang area were of a more serious nature and were difficult of solution. The Tawang monastery's practice of hiring the services of the Tsona Dzongpons, which the British had allowed to continue on the basis of assurances given by Lonchen Shatra in 1914, had now led to the inevitable complications. From the position of subordinates of the Tawang monastery (which was their real position according to the accounts of Nain Singh, Bailey, and Lonchen Shatra), the Dzongpons had now emerged, apparently with encouragement from Lhasa, as parallel authorities and had started levying dues independently of the monastery. Since the Government of Tibet had never repudiated the 1914 agreement and had on the other hand reaffirmed it as late as 1935 (on the occasion of a tour undertaken by Kingdon Ward in Tibetan territory adjoining the "McMahon Line"), the activities of the Tsona Dzongpons were *prima facie* illegal.

It was easy to put an end to this by stationing a Political Officer in Tawang as was first suggested by Bell and McMahon n 1914. The Assam Government reminded the Government of India that the time had come to put this suggestion into effect. The Government of India agreed as a preliminary measure to send an expedition under Captain Light-foot in 1938, but were unable to follow this up by more permanent arrangements due to financial stringency and the outbreak of war in 1939. The illegal activities of the Dzongpons, therefore, continued. After 1945 these activities were gradually put an end to, and in 1951 a Political Officer came to be stationed in Tawang. It appears that this action was delayed not because the government had any doubts regarding the illegal nature of Tibetan activities but because it thought that its position in the areas nearer to Chinese territories proper having been consolidated, there would be little difficulty in dealing with Tibet in regard to areas further west.

Except in Tawang and the upper Dihong valley, there was no Tibetan activity elsewhere on the frontier. But there were other factors to be considered. The Chinese had revived their interest in Tibet and there were signs that after the war they would renew their efforts to re-establish their authority. In that event the system of tribal autonomy and the policy of non-interference adopted by the British Government with the best of intentions towards the frontier areas might be misconstrued as lack of administration and tempt the Chinese to renew encroachments similar to those they had tried in 1912 in the Walong area. To prevent this it was necessary not only to establish more posts nearer the frontier but to intensify control over the tribes. This the Government of India started doing after 1943. Not only were more posts established but a number of special officers sent to tour the interior in an effort to understand the conditions and the cultural background of the tribal people. These efforts were accelerated after 1950 when it was found that earlier fears about the Chinese were not without basis and that in fact the Chinese were probing the frontier in a number of areas. By the time the Chinese completed their occupation of Tibet, the Government of India were firmly in possession of the entire frontier area. Whether it would have been better to take measures of consolidation earlier than were actually taken seems to be too academic a matter to discuss at the present moment. What is important is that the Chinese Government who were perfectly aware of the stages by which Indian administration was intensified never questioned its legal basis and it was apparently due to reasons entirely extraneous to the territorial question that they thought fit to raise a dispute in 1959.

10

Some Conclusions

WESTERN SECTOR

CERTAIN BASIC POINTS emerge from this analysis of the evolution of the Sino-Indian boundary. The claims put forward by China in the Western Sector have had no historical basis whatsoever. West of the Karakoram pass, the Mir of Hunza and the Kashmir Government had exercised authority over a considerable area south of the Kuen Lun. After 1890, due to reasons of policy and strategy, the British relinquished some of these claims and induced the Chinese authorities to extend their jurisdiction. Accordingly, the Chinese started occupying the area and succeeded by 1947 in establishing their authority up to the Mustagh and the Aghil ranges. Later, Pakistan who had been in illegal occupation of the Hunza area confirmed, in her agreement with China, the boundary along the Mustagh, but surrendered the rights over the area lying between the Aghil and the Karakoram ranges.

In the region east of the Karakoram pass, the British were not inhibited by reasons of policy and strategy. On the other hand, in view of the trade routes which traversed this region, they had evinced considerable interest and established their rights very early through explorations and surveys in the 1860s. Later, their failure to find convenient routes resulted, for a time, in the region being neglected. It appeared that some British officials at the end of the nineteenth century were inclined, because of their ignorance of the real traditional limits, to relinquish Indian rights over a part of this region. However, after 1912, this policy changed and the British authorities reasserted their rights. The Chinese always considered the Kuen Lun as their boundary in this region and never took any interest in the area south of it. By 1947, therefore, the area continued to be in Indian possession.

The suggestion put forward by Lamb for a compromise line along what he calls the MacDonald-Macartney line is based not on the strength of Chinese claims but on the sole basis that a proposal had been made in 1899 along such a line. However, we have seen how little justification there was for this proposal and how it had neither historical nor geographical basis. In fact it had been abandoned by the Government of India long ago. The fact is that south of the Kuen Lun there is no continuous range which can be considered an effective barrier or a boundary. The so-called Lak Tsung range, which is supposed to form the Indus-Tarim watershed, does not exist on the ground. In a mountainous and uninhabited area, unless a boundary follows easily recognizable and prominent features, it ceases to have any value.

The MacDonald Line does not leave the Aksai Chin road on the Chinese side, as Lamb has assumed. It cuts the road some miles west of 80°E Longitude. Actually, the question of the road is of little importance in the consideration of the boundary problem here. India has offered the use of the road for civilian purposes, and China has shown little interest. From the latter's point of view, evidently the occupation of Aksai Chin is important for reasons other than that of the road, for had it only been a question of communications, she would have easily cleared another track east of 80°E Longitude along the Keria-Polu route which was in fact the traditional route between Rudok and Khotan.

The eastern boundary of Ladakh with Tibet had never presented any problem. In 1924 the question of ownership of a few pastures in the region east of the Pangong lake had been discussed between India and Tibet, but there had been no dispute regarding the Lanak pass, Spanggur, and Demchok areas. The boundary, in these areas, had always been well known and the Chinese themselves had resisted British attempts to redefine or demarcate this boundary. Unlike in the Aksai Chin area, this is a region which is inhabited and for which travel accounts and administrative records including survey and revenue reports are available. It is easy, after a careful examination of such evidence, to arrive at definite conclusions. The main points along this boundary which happen to lie along the routes normally used are the Lanak pass at the head of the Chang Chenmo, Niagzu in the Pangong region, and Demchok near the Indus. Once the position of the boundary along these points is determined, it is easy to draw the rest of the alignment. In regard to all these three points, the Indian side produced overwhelming amount of evidence which included references from travellers' accounts, survey reports, and revenue reports. The Chinese produced nothing of the sort.[1]

MIDDLE SECTOR

In the Middle Sector, there had really been no territorial dispute between India and Tibet in the past. Indeed, in the Spiti and Shipki areas, there had never been any dispute nor friction of any type. In the area of Barahoti (an insignificant patch of territory of not more than three to four square miles) there had been no dispute but only a controversy whether Tibetan officials could come into Indian territory for the purpose of taxing their traders. There was a similar controversy in the Nilang-Jadhang area. These matters had been discussed between Indian and Tibetan officials in 1890, 1914, and 1926, but neither side had been inclined to give much importance to them. The Barahoti question was discussed also between Indian and Chinese officials in 1958 and a partial agreement reached. China has, of late, recognized that most of the areas disputed by it in this sector have been in the actual control of India. Provided there is a basic desire on the part of the Chinese to settle the issues in a reasonable manner, it is unlikely that these controversies will present much difficulty.

[1]The evidence of Kashmir Atlas of 1868, to which Lamb has made reference (p. 173), cannot by any means overweigh that of revenue reports.

EASTERN SECTOR

In the Eastern Sector, it is now generally recognized that the claims put forward by the Chinese to the vast areas up to the *Inner Line* are absurd and without basis. Neither the *Inner Line* nor the so-called *Outer Line* had any thing to do with the real traditional international boundary. Except for the stray incursions of 1911-12 in a remote corner of this area, the Chinese had had nothing to do with the area at any time in history. They cannot base their claims on Tibetan rights either, for, in the major part of this area, Tibet exercised neither political jurisdiction nor cultural influence at any time. In a few border tracts such as Tawang, upper Dihong valley, and Walong, although there had been certain misconceptions earlier regarding the nature of Tibetan influence that prevailed there, these had been cleared as a result of the investigations conducted during the years 1911-14 and Tibet had accepted, through the agreement of 1914, that the influence she exerted and the rights she exercised in these areas were of a non-political nature. In view of these it is difficult to see how there can be any talk of territorial adjustment in this area.

The objections of the Chinese to the agreement of 1914 have no validity. Whether China accepts it or not the world recognizes that Tibet had, before 1951, been practically independent and that she had always exercised treaty-making powers. This is the conclusion which the International Commission of Jurists has also arrived at. It would be unrealistic, therefore, to expect India to cut the ground off her own feet by invalidating the Indo-Tibetan Agreement of 1914.

THE REAL PROBLEM

Evidence of China's behaviour hitherto suggests that she does not view the problem as one affecting the boundary alone. In her dealings with Burma and the Soviet Union, she has demonstrated that she is capable of relinquishing shadowy claims over

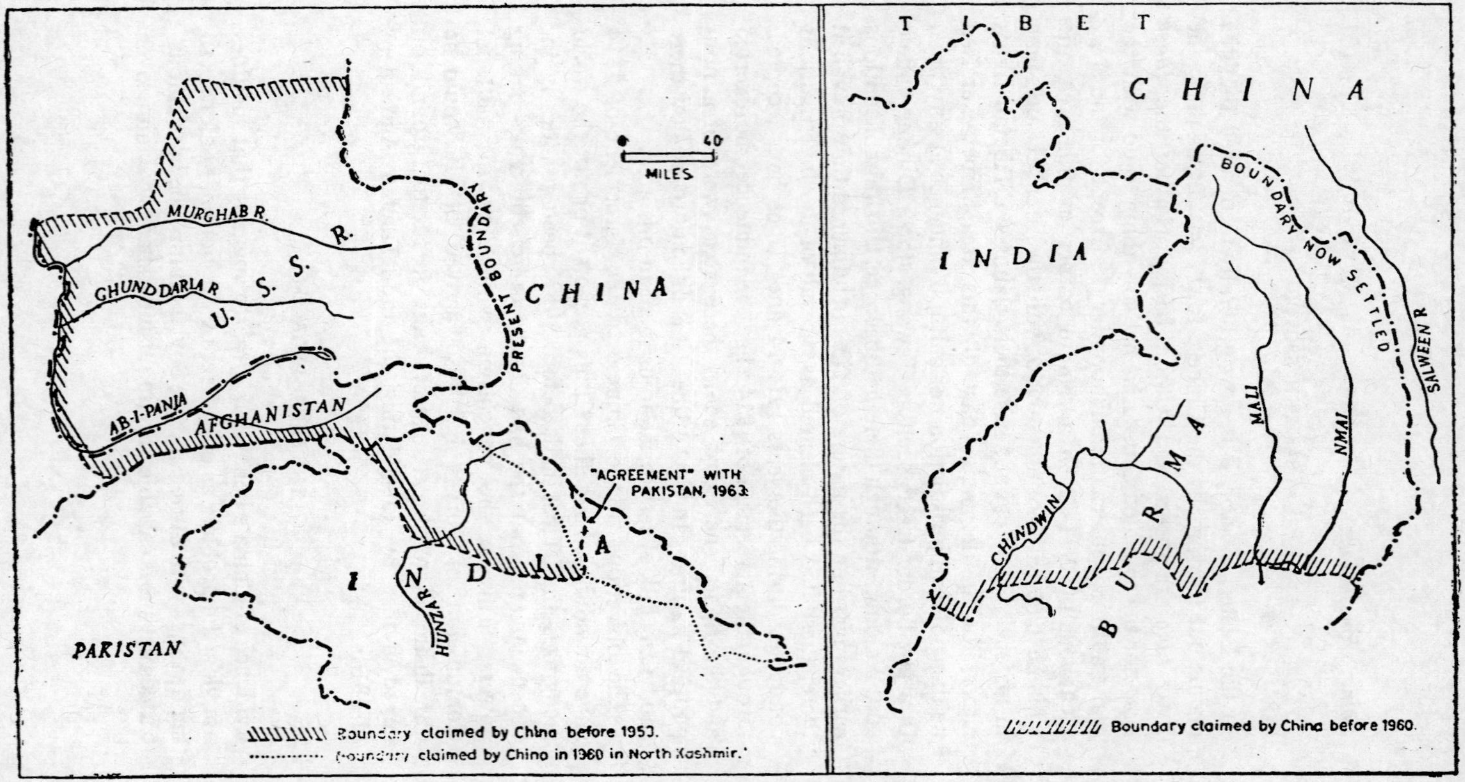

MAP 7. Showing Chinese claims, now relinquished, against USSR, Afghanistan, and Burma

large territories (see Map 7). The claims against India, which are no less shadowy, would perhaps have similarly been relinquished had they not, in the meantime, been involved with other aims. In 1954 and 1956, China had given specific assurances that her maps were not to be taken seriously as they were mere copies of Kuomintang maps, and that she would take a reasonable and realistic view of the India-China boundary question. However, by 1959, apparently due to changes in her general outlook and global designs, she effected a change in this attitude. It is outside the scope of this work to analyze the factors underlying this change, but it is relevant to point out that China herself has related it to ideological and power factors. If that is so, it seems too naive and superficial to assume that China would have responded to compromise offers or that such compromises would have mitigated the extent of her hostility towards India. Indeed, China's recent *volte face* against Burma proves the contrary, for Burma had not only settled her boundary with China but made exceptional efforts to maintain friendly relations with her. India made several attempts to come to a reasonable understanding. She was not only willing, right from the beginning, to discuss minor adjustments in the boundary but made concrete proposals from time to time to pave the way for such discussions. In November 1959, she suggested neutralization of the disputed area in northern Ladakh pending settlement. Later, she offered the use of the Aksai Chin road for civilian purposes. As late as September 1962, India suggested a definite date (15 October 1962) for holding negotiations. China rejected all these and launched her massive invasion in a bid to occupy the areas claimed by her. The efforts made by the six friendly Afro-Asian countries to relieve the tension caused by this invasion and to restore the *status quo* as a basis for future negotiations were turned down. Even offers made by India to refer the dispute to the International Court or to arbitration were rejected.

The inevitable conclusion one reaches is that if the India-China border problem is still unresolved it is not because of any lack of efforts on the Indian side to settle it on a reasonable basis, but because of deeper and more complex factors underlying Chinese international policies. The great controversy—both internal and external—in which China has been involved during the last few years has brought to light many facets of these policies and laid bare, in a manner never known hitherto, the complex and intricate working of the Chinese mind in the pursuit of its objectives—both national and international—and its ambitions in both the ideological and power spheres. There have been differences in the leadership regarding the methods of achieving these objectives, but not in regard to the objectives themselves. The quest for power and the urge for domination seem to be qualities basic to the current Chinese leadership—both Maoist and anti-Maoist. There may be transformations and there may be vicissitudes caused by internal strife and politics, but the basic urges and qualities characteristic of "Sino-centrism" will remain for a long time until perhaps changes in the power balance compel it again to go into another of its periodical hibernations. It is in the understanding of this basic position and devising proper means of meeting it in its various transformations and manifestations that the solution of the India-China border dispute, and indeed of most other problems created by China in this part of the world, lies.

Appendix

Correspondence showing Russian Government's concurrence to the Convention of 1914 (refer to text on p. 19):

Telegram P., dated the 26th (received 27th) May 1914.[1]
From—His Majesty's Secretary of State for India, London.
To—His Excellency the Viceroy, Simla.

Tibet. Please refer to your telegram, dated the 21st instant. His Majesty's Government did not feel that they were in a position to decide so important a matter at such a short notice, and British Ambassador at St. Petersburgh was accordingly instructed on 22nd instant as follows:

"His Majesty's Government agree to deletion of Article 10 and its replacement by article declaring that English text is authoritative. With regard to Articles 6 and 8, His Majesty's Government would be prepared to address an official note to Russian Government stating that until His Majesty's Government have come to an understanding with the Russian Government they will not act on provisions of these articles. If the tripartite Convention be published, His Majesty's Government would be prepared to make public at the same time the above official note. Pending the conclusion of understanding with Russian Government on the points referred to above, His Majesty's Government would not require any secret engagements as proposed by the Russian Minister for Foreign Affairs, and His Majesty's Government would in fact treat the Convention of 1907 as binding on them and in full force. On the above conditions I hope Russian Minister for Foreign Affairs will enter no objection to His Majesty's Government proceeding to sign tripartite Convention as the rights of Russian Government will be preserved in entirety and no parts of the tripartite Convention will be put into force by His Majesty's Government which in any way clash with 1907 Convention until such time as a complete understanding has been reached between the Governments of Russia and Great Britain."

Following is Buchanan's reply, dated 24th May:

"Russian Minister for Foreign Affairs said that he would prefer that tripartite Convention should not be signed until such time as we had definitely accepted proposed arrangement. He eventually agreed on my explaining risks which such a delay would involve, to our signing Con-

[1]Extract from Proc. 290 in File S.E, October 1914, 134-396,

vention at once, provided that Article 10 be deleted as proposed and that His Majesty's Government addressed official note at once in which they engage not to give effect to provisions of Articles 6 and 8 without a previous understanding with Russian Government. He begged, however, that Convention should not be made public until understanding had been arrived at on the whole question between the two Governments. There could be no object, said he, for immediate publication of Convention, and he hoped, in the circumstances, that we would consent to keep it confidential for the time being while he would keep confidential the note which we were to address to him."

Telegram P., dated the 8th (received 9th) June 1914.[2]
From—His Majesty's Secretary of State for India, London.
To—His Excellency the Viceroy, Simla.

China-Tibet Negotiations. On 6th June, His Majesty's Ambassador at St. Petersburgh was instructed as follows:

"You may now inform Russian Government that an exchange of notes, both public and secret, with regard to Article 6 and Article 8 of Tripartite Convention, drafted on lines suggested in your telegram No. 117, is agreed to by His Majesty's Government."

* * * *

"Your Excellency may immediately proceed to an exchange of notes embodying this arrangement, if it proves satisfactory to the Russian Government."

[2]Extract from Proc. 303 in File S.E. October 1914, 134-396.